Who am I?

Louis Godschalk

Who am I?

Aspekt Publishers

Who am I?
© 2019 Louis Godschalk
© 2019 Aspekt Publishers
Aspekt Publishers | Amersfoortsestraat 27
3769 AD Soesterberg | The Netherlands
info@uitgeverijaspekt.nl | www.uitgeverijaspekt.nl
Coverdesign: Mark Heuveling & Snezhina Uzunova
Lay-out: Paul Timmerman

ISBN: 978-94-6338-554-1
NUR: 680

Disclaimer – The author and the publisher have made every feasible effort to determine and acquire copyright permissions for material presented in this book. If any right-holders have been overlooked we kindly request them to apply to the publisher.

Contents

Why I am telling you my life story   7

1   From Amsterdam to Scharnegoutum   12
2   Decisions with far-reaching consequences   16
3   From warm to cold   36
4   What everyone knew, except me   39
5   1956: The year of the truth   43
6   From the village to the city   47
7   On my own two feet   49
8   The crucial years   52
9   1964: The year of the awareness   61
10 'What does it mean for us to be Jewish?'   74
11 The new life   80
12 You are not alone   89
13 Chasing trails   92
14 The incomprehensible reality of Auschwitz   100
15 These are the names   106
16 Getting to the bottom of things   111
17 A never-ending movie starts all over again   116
18 Completing the circle   120
19 Stolpersteine   125
20 Questions and answers   128
21 We count our blessings   130

Words of gratitude and appreciation   134

Annexes:

1	A vision	137
2	From generation to generation	139
3	In memoriam Hendrika Rienstra-Oosterkamp	141
4	In memoriam for my 'mama'	143
5	The kaddish prayer	148
6	Yad Vashem award	150
7	What will be the new home of the Jewish hidden child	157
8	Genealogy of the Godschalk and Zwaaf families	164
9	Max Abram	166
10	Jacques Grishaver	169
11	Memories of Nida and Louis Blok-Blitz	171
12	Simon Meerschwam	176

Names and definitions* 178

Index of names 207

Consulted sources 217

B"H*

Why I am telling you my life story

Shalom dear mother Anna
Shalom dear father Lion

Shalom dear grandfather Louis Godschalk
Shalom dear grandmother Cornelia Godschalk

Shalom dear grandfather Hartog Zwaaf
Shalom dear grandmother Clara Zwaaf

Shalom dear uncles, aunts, nieces and nephews
Shalom my dear Godschalk and Zwaaf family

Shalom to all of you, I hoped for more than 60 years
that one of you would knock on my door one day

Shalom, it was made impossible for me to even to say Shalom to you
Because you were brutally murdered by men and women

You are dead, and I am alive.

This book is dedicated to you, my murdered parents and my family. Parents provide the generational link that ties their child to their cultural traditions and fundamental values. Honoring my parents means honoring the traditions they once represented. I was still a baby when you were all inhumanely murdered.

From an orphaned Jewish hidden child in the Netherlands to a citizen of Israel. From a Jewish War orphan, alone on the world, to a proud Jewish (grand)father.

Moshe* was the ultimate Jewish Hidden Child, sent off in a basket by his mother hoping to be rescued from his Jewish fate.

This action robbed Moshe from his identity twice, first as a new born, and again when he discovered his 'other' Jewish identity. Moshe struggled to discover himself in a world of changing realities. It is axiomatic that Jewish Children* hidden during the Second World War* share this history with Moshe, as they went into hiding as Jews* and returned to a world in which they were unaware of their Jewish identity.

'Hidden children' is the term given to those like me, who were of tender years during the Shoah*. We managed to survive because good, brave people took us in and hid us away. We were sometimes literally hidden, as we were kept out of sight.

For me, the Shoah is not only part of the past, but also of the present, it will also stay with me in the future. The memories of this tragedy will remain with me for my whole life. I, as a child survivor, could not save my family and my loved ones from the flames that engulfed them. By telling my story, I want to commemorate the Shoah, its victims, the resistance* and rescuers who sometimes paid with their lives. To prevent these martyrs from being forgotten, to keep history from being distorted, or the truth fading away.

I want to thank and honor the Righteous Dutch People who risked their lives to rescue me, a Jewish baby, during one of the most horrendous, tragic periods in our Jewish history. I am deeply grateful and admire the handful of men and women who had the moral and physical hardihood to defy the brutal ordinance of the German tyrant and saved countless Jews under the threat of the firing squad. Nobody could imagine that this Second World War* would mean such awful disaster for Jews, the loss of a third of our Jewish people in a conflict which we did not instigate, to which we were no party.

Even today, my mind cannot grasp the motives for this unspeakable, premeditated barbarity, or, above all, what good this mass murder of Jews could have brought the German people. How could it happen in a Christian, civilized and secure country like the Netherlands, with its government in London? Jews were humiliated, disguised robbed. 102,000 Jews, citizens of the Netherlands, were brutally murdered by one or more fellow human beings.

I had no chance of survival in 1942. As a Jewish Hidden Child survivor of the Shoah,* I myself did in no way contribute to my survival during the Second World War. I feel like I am setting out to do the impossible in trying to explain my thoughts, my hopes and how I tried to realize these to you Strive to give you a brief overview of my past. I write this book because the Age of Shoah* Survivors is drawing to a close.

Soon, there will no longer be any survivors who can say: 'I am a Second World* war (Jewish Hidden Child) survivor'. The time has come that nobody will be able to tell and write about his 'Shoah Survival'. All that will be left will be literature, research, picture, films and multitudinous testimony. The dark inheritance and feelings of the Shoah, which was so indelibly stamped on my soul and my heart once, will end.

The great thunder of the Second World War was silenced in the spring of 1945. In the eerie silence that followed, I, one of the vestiges of Dutch Jewry, emerged from hiding, orphaned, with no close relatives. When I grew up, I did not turn into a bitter person, only seeking vengeance. Ivonne and I married in 1964, and in 1981 we chose to rebuild our Jewish life in Israel, our only Jewish State. My aliyah*, together with my dear partner for life, Ivonne, our daughter, Anna Vanessa (1969) and our son, Lion Patrick (1973) were how I existentially rose up from the Shoah*.

The foundations of the State of Israel were built not only on the memory of our six million murdered Jewish people but kept the historical lessons of the Shoah in mind, ensuring that a Jewish Shoah will never happen again. The Shoah did not only destroy six million of our people but also six million worlds, each one precious beyond description. Now it is no longer 1290, when England decided to evict the Jews*. Now it is no longer 1492, when Spain decided that Jews could leave, convert or burn at the stake.

Now it is no longer 1930, when Germany turned from a land of seemingly limitless Jewish opportunity into a state with the destructive plan to eradicate our people. Israel has repeatedly demonstrated that Jews can effectively protect themselves since 1948.

Remember, preserve never forget!
Remembering – zachor*,
preserving/respecting – shamor*.
The command to remember,
to preserve
is absolute
in Jewish tradition.

This is why I started writing you, my dear wife, children, grandchildren and friends, to pass the torch of the memory of the lost and murdered Jewish generation on to you. My writings will not be a scholarly, historical account. I write about my past, what this past did to and with me. I try to be objective and will not attempt to explain what has happened and why it happened.

This story is about my life during and after the Second World War. This story is about my life with Ivonne, our life with our children and grandchildren. This story is about a Jewish baby, who was separated from his parents, from his Jewish family, from his Jewish culture, from his Jewish tradition, from the Jewish way of life, and nearly from his Jewish future. This story is about the past of a Jewish baby and what this past did to him. This story is about my troubled identity, my fears, my hopes. This story is about and tells you about my torn identity, in which I did not know that I was a Jew until I was 13 years old. This story is about and tells you about my fears. My hope when I received this unbelievable information. This story is about my past, written in the present, taking a glance at the future. This story is about and connected/inextricably linked to my dear partner Ivonne, my lovely wife, the endless source of support given by Ivonne, my partner for life. This story is about and how I tried to write down from memory, it is not a scholarly account. This story is about a Jewish baby who did not receive the basic right to be brought up in his own culture, to be educated by his own parents. This is my personal story as I remember it, so please bear in mind that my memory has its limitations.

I try to stick to the truth. The events that form the background of this story are part of my personal history. After the Second World War, I saw things through the eyes of a young child. I live in the present; I look at the past to describe it. Keep this in mind while reading. I write from the depths of my heart. If, in the end, you do not understand everything that I wrote, do not be surprised, as I still have that same problem.

Allow me to start with where it all began!

1

From Amsterdam to Scharnegoutum

I was born in Amsterdam, in the Netherlands, on November 1, 1942, at Réaumurstraat 22 to be precise. All Dutch Jews were in danger at that time. In July 1943, shortly before my parents were deported to Westerbork from the Hollandsche Schouwburg, my parents took the emotional, heroic decision to hand me over to the Dutch Resistance*, which tried to save Jewish children* from deportation. My parents gave them permission to find a family for me where I could hide and survive the war, to later be reunited with my parents. Westerbork was a transit camp from which people were sent to the Nazi extermination camps in the 'East'. More than one hundred thousand Jews went towards their doom through this 'Judendurchgangslager'.

1940. Amsterdam Réaumurstraat 22, my grandmother and my father.
I was born above the shop

I went from hiding place to hiding place from the beginning of July 1943 until April 14, 1944. That was the day on which Mr. Stroop, active in the Resistance, a member of the National Organization for Assistance to People in Hiding (LO*) knocked on the door of the Oosterkamp* family in Scharnegoutum, a village near Sneek. He was holding an 18-month old Jewish baby, called Gerrit, on his arm. Hennie not only opened the door but also her heart. My times of wandering were over. This would be my last hiding address.

The Oosterkamp family lived in one of the houses of the dairy plant on the Zwette, the canal between Sneek and Leeuwarden. My 'family' at that time consisted of Klaas Oosterkamp (1889), his daughters Hennie (1919) Eke (1930), his sons Marten (1921) Siebe (1923), and me. The wife of Klaas Oosterkamp, Ruurdje Boersma, had died in 1941, Hennie now took care of the housekeeping. She also took care of me. I am certain that I was very lucky in this respect, as she had a golden loving character. The National Organization for Assistance to People in Hiding (LO)* provided compensation for my subsistence, clothing, food stamps. Hennie told me, at the end of the fifties, that I called her 'mama' when I was lying on the table to be changed for the first time. Mama was one of the few words I spoke when I arrived at the Oosterkamp family.

A lot of Scharnegoutum residents, as in many other places in Friesland, were active in the Resistance*. A German civil servant later called Scharnegoutum 'Das Terroristendorf' due to the many acts of resistance. The 'Oosterkamps' were no exception. They knew that protecting a Jewish baby was dangerous. Not only Klaas Oosterkamp but also his sons Marten, Siebe and their half-brother Thomas Boersma were active in the Dutch Resistance.

The mother of Klaas his deceased wife, Eelkje Boersma, already well into her eighties, also did her bit. People who had to 'disappear' for a few days could always knock on her door and stay as long as necessary. The old woman knew how to step up to the plate. Two (Dutch) police officers once asked her whether she was hiding Jews in her house. She convincingly, calmly answered: 'No, there are no Jews hidden here, just take a look upstairs!' after which the men left. Eelkje Boersma also hid crew members of downed Allied aircraft until a specialized Resistance organization helped them flee to unoccupied France or neutral Spain. She received an award for this from General Eisenhower after the war.

People in Scharnegoutum were aware of the dangers of Nazism. It hosted a department of De Bijzondere Vrijwillige Landstorm (BVL), just like a number of other villages. This was a semi-military organization, founded in 1918. The goal was to defend the Kingdom of the Netherlands against domestic riots. The lists of members kept from 1919 to 1936 show that Klaas Oosterkamp was a member of this BVL during this period.

A number of dangerous situations occurred. Mama told me years later that I was taken in a rowing boat across the Zwettekanaal to another house once, where I lived with the Jukema family in the attic of their house for a few days. I could sometimes see Tippie Koeke from the attic window. This is what I called uncle Thomas Boersma, a half-brother of Hennie, who was a baker's assistant and delivered bread. He always gave me a piece of cake when he saw me. Another time, Hennie's brother Marten and his fiancé Minke took me to Mastenbroek in a rowing boat, a hamlet on a dead-end path from the Sint Martensdyk. We stayed the night in the boat and returned home the next morning, once the 'all clear' signal was given. One of our neighbors was the Wiersma family. Gerlof Foppe Wiersma and his brother Sjoerd, who lived in Joure, were active in the Resistance. They hid people in their house and served as a refuge for people in need of an address to hide at.

Mama took care of me and gradually became attached to me. Her brothers and sister also gave me love and attention. They hugged me. There was peace, joy and laughter in the Oosterkamp residence, despite the war. They had enough milk and dairy products as Klaas Oosterkamp worked at the dairy factory.

It was the 5th of May 1945 and peace had finally come. The Oosterkamp family did not hear anything about my own family. For the time being, I stayed where I was. Mama did not want to give me up either, as she had grown attached to me. There was also a real boom in marriages, which usually had been postponed. Klaas Oosterkamp wanted to remarry with the widow Klaske Hofstra. Klaske brought two adult daughters with her. Klaske agreed to come and live with her two daughters with Klaas Oosterkamp and his three children. She did not want to take care of the little Jewish boy. Fortunately, Hennie was about to marry Feike Rienstra* (1922). I would go with Hennie and Feike and live with them until I would be reunited with my own family. Hennie and Feike married on November 8, 1945. Klaas Oosterkamp and Klaske Hofstra married the week after.

As a 3-year old toddler, I did not know what happened around me. Hennie remained my mama and Feike became my father. I will call them my foster parents from now on, based on a court ruling. When I refer to my grandparents, I am talking about the parents of Hennie and Feike.

My suffering was by no means over on May 5, 1945. It was about to begin. A new situation arose, which caused me to become very disoriented. This was partly due to the decision of the OPK (Commission for War Foster Children) (Annex 7).

2

Decisions with far-reaching consequences

The Chuppah* (Jewish wedding ceremony) of my parents Lion Godschalk* and Anna Zwaaf (Annex 9) was held on Wednesday, the 5th of June 1940. The Netherlands had just been occupied. The first shock, especially among the Jewish population, had subsided as 'little happened' so far, but the prospects for the young couple were not exactly positive. My parents had a store in household goods and my father also worked as an architectural broker. They lived as religious Jews. Their store was closed on Sabbath*.

Wedding picture of my parents Lion Godschalk and Anna Zwaaf

My sister Cornelia was born on August 31, 1941. She was named after my father's mother, Cornelia Godschalk-Jacobs.

A disaster occurred on January 3, 1942. It was winter, my mother hung the laundry to dry at the stove in the living room above the shop. She had gone downstairs to help customers. Upstairs, the laundry caught fire and my sister suffocated in the smoke. The grief and guilt of my parents must have been unimaginable! I was born ten months later, and another eight months later they said goodbye to me and went towards their own doom. I cannot describe their marriage period any clearer.

I was circumcised on the eighth day after my birth. This Brit Milah* was celebrated at home. My parents went into hiding with me after my birth, together with my grandparents Louis and Cornelia Godschalk-Jacobs. They were not the only ones of my extended family who had gone into hiding. I learned this at the end of the fifties, thanks to my mother's nanny, 'aunt' Bettie and her husband 'uncle' Max Cosman*. They told me that an uncle on my mother's side, Hartog Zwaaf, paid the costs of the daily subsistence for all the family members in hiding. Hartog Zwaaf had to hastily leave his hiding place and flee, leaving his jacket with his wallet still in his pocket. The people hiding my parents, my grandparent and me, did not want to grant them any credit and betrayed us to Jew hunters (bounty hunters*). They received 7.50 guilders (called *kopgeld* in Dutch) for each reported Jew. At the end of the war, when there were fewer and fewer Jews left, this amount was increased to 40 guilders. We were locked up in the Hollandsche Schouwburg at the Plantage Middenlaan in Amsterdam, near Artis (the Zoo). It used to be called the Joodsche Schouwburg.

The 'Joodsche Schouwburg' was opened in 1941. Only Jews were allowed to perform, and attend shows there. The performances came to an end on July 18, 1942. The building was to serve as a collection and deportation site for arrested Jews. The name was also changed to Hollandsche Schouwburg. Groups of Jews were transported to the Westerbork transit camp in Drenthe from here. The Hollandsche Schouwburg was overcrowded, chaotic, and noisy. All chairs had been removed, the 'guests' were lying down or sitting on the floor and the sanitary facilities were far from sufficient. They could go outside once a day. In one year, approximately 60,000 people had 'gone' through the Hollandsche Schouwburg. The staff of the Hollandsche Schouwburg consisted of Jews.

The director, Walter Süskind* (1906-1945), was given permission by the Germans to let children under thirteen stay in the nursery* opposite the Hollandsche Schouwburg. This made the nursery part of the Hollandsche Schouwburg. The nursery was guarded less strictly than the Hollandsche Schouwburg. Süskind and his staff were masters in forging deportation lists.

The nursery opened up a new escape route in the spring of 1943. The Hervormde Kweekschool (Protestant Teacher College) was two doors from the nursery, at number 27. The gardens of the building were adjacent to each other behind the middle building.

Child rescuers could enter the school and leave with a child in a backpack or large shopping bag under the eye of the Germans.

Walter Süskind had an unbridled energy, was resourceful, and always found new ways to deceive the Germans. He was a tower of strength, an example for all those who worked to save as many Jewish children* and adults from deportation as possible.

The vast majority of Jewish parents was approached by one of the three nurses appointed by Miss Pimentel, the director of the nursery: Sieny Kattenburg, Betty Oudkerk, or Fanny Philips. My parents will undoubtedly also have been approached by one of these three ladies to make the difficult heroic decision to 'temporarily' hand me over to Hester van Lennep*, the later wife of Sandor Baracs*. Both were also involved in the Trouw resistance group.

My parents took this tough decision in the hope that we would be reunited after the war. After first having first buried their daughter Cornelia, they had gone into hiding for a while before being betrayed. It is unimaginable what they, and all others who were chased by the

Nazis, had to endure before they were murdered. It is heart wrenching. My parents gave me a chance to survive and live for a second time.

My parents and grandparents, Louis and Cornelia Godschalk-Jacobs, were, together with my parents, transported to the Westerbork transit camp from the Hollandsche Schouwburg on July 17, 1943. They stayed there in barrack 97 for three days. Freight trains filled with 2,209 Jews departed from Westerbork on July 20, 1943. These people were transported like cattle in wagons under inhumane conditions. Among them were my father, mother, and grandparents. This train arrived in the hell of the extermination camp called Sobibor* three days later. They were gassed immediately after they arrived.

The OPK, the Commission for War Foster Children, was founded by Royal Decree on August 13, 1945. As the director of the OPK, Mr. Sandor Baracs* was responsible for my post-war identification procedure. My parents were murdered, the OPK had to submit a custody recommendation to the court. This custody was the start of a battle within the OPK. The majority of its members were non-Jews. It turned into a struggle for the Jewish minority, a struggle they sadly could not win.

We first got in touch with Mr. and Mrs. Baracs in 1965 and this continued till they both passed away. I asked something about my rescue from the nursery when visiting them in Doesburg at the end of August 1980. He assumed that my OPK file would contain an answer to my question. Mr. Baracs gave me the address of the OPK archive. I wrote them a letter and was invited to read my file at their offices. I was hesitant to open it. What would I find? Would I be able to handle it? After this brief hesitation, I opened the file. After skimming through it, I was given permission to take my OPK file home with me.

The notes showed that Baracs (resistance name: uncle Piet) had received a thousand guilders from my father. Not to save his son, but as a contribution to the costs of his resistance group. The money came from my uncle Hartog de Hoop, who was married to my aunt

Hendrika Godschalk. Hartog de Hoop also gave fifteen thousand guilders of the family to Mr. H.G.A. van Leeuwen to be kept safe, as his brother H.L. van Leeuwen was the bookkeeper of the Godschalk family. These data confirmed earlier suspicions that I was the child of wealthy parents and family. The file is unclear about what happened to me between July 1943 and the beginning of 1944.

I will include the main OPK file comments here:

September 2, 1945:
Miss H. Oosterkamp writes: 'That she has been taking care of a Jewish boy now of about two and a half years old during the occupation from the 14th of April 1944 since his parents are no longer there and she is very attached to the child, and the child to her. She would like to remain the guardian of this child.'

September 27, 1945:
On the forms provided by the OPK, Miss Hennie Oosterkamp* lists the following, among other things: 'Brought to me on April 14, 1944 by Mr. Stroop, Kloosterhof Sneek. By bike. My father registered earlier, to become a foster family for a young child, with Mr. G.F. Wiersma, Rijksstraatweg, Scharnegoutum, in February 1944. His first name is Gerrit, which I believe is false because he is of Jewish descent. I am not aware of his information and the addresses of the family before he was brought to us. Upon his arrival, Mr. Stroop did not tell us anything that could help identify him. He could speak a few words in Dutch when he arrived at us. We are in contact with the LO*.' They provide the Oosterkamp family with vouchers.

Without date:
OPK memo: File number unknown. Child born in 1943. Address: Mrs. N. Oosterkamp, Scharnegoutum (Fr). References: Van der Goot, Grootzand 57. First foster parents. K. Dijkstra, Sacramentstraat Sneek. Still living family members. Contact: Mien Bouman, Westeinde 17. From the nursery*. Miss Oosterkamp takes care of the housekeeping for her father. She has been engaged for five years and will take the

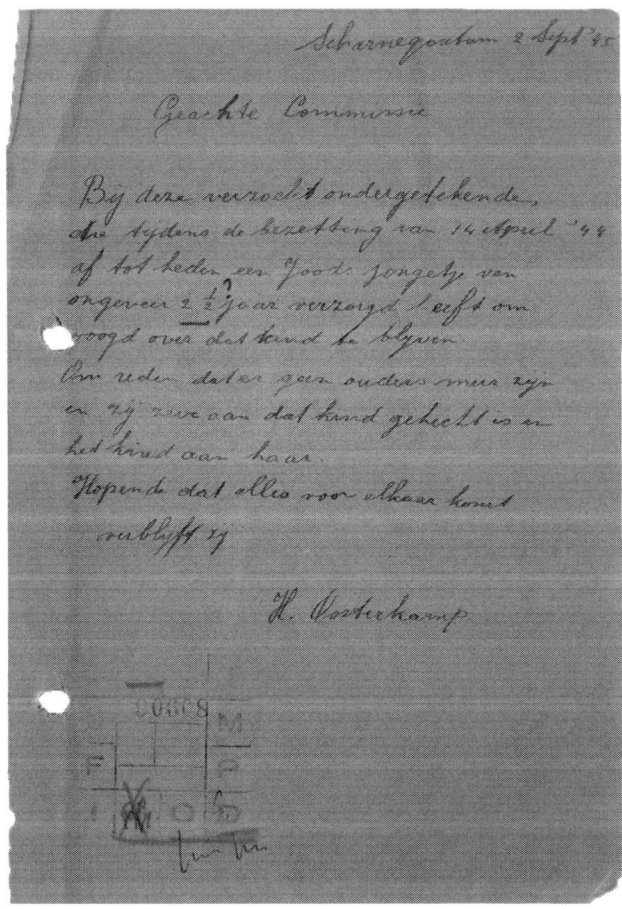
Request for custody

child she is attached to with her once she marries. It is not exactly a civilized environment, yet the child had a good upbringing there.

October 2, 1945:
The OPK stamped this information and my file is given number 100201.

October 24, 1945:
A letter to Miss H. Oosterkamp, signed by 'The Director': *'Did you maybe have two children, Gerrie and Gerrit, in your home, the youngest of whom went to another address?'*

Request for custody signed by H. Oosterkamp, send to the OPK,
The Guardianship Committee for Foster War Children

October 28, 1945:
Miss H. Oosterkamp repeats what she had written on September 27. She adds: 'That she took care of a child. *Maybe two forms have been completed, or else I don't understand the question about two children. My name is Oosterkamp, not Aartenkamp.*'

November 15, 1945:
G.M. Meijer (Resistance Group Sneek) sends the following to the OPK: 'In response to your letter to the Van der Groot family, Grootzand 57 in Sneek, the following: The indicated child 'Gerrit' was placed temporarily with them in August 1943.'

March ?, 1946:
Almelo, Mrs. M. Bouman contacts the OPK, Documentation Department: 'To my regret, I must inform you in response to your letter of February 12, 1946 that I don't know of any details about the war foster child Gerrit, who is being cared for by Miss Oosterkamp in Scharnegoutum. Yours sincerely, M. Bouman.'

March 15, 1946:
Administrator I. Zwaaf, sends a number of names and addresses of the still living Godschalk and Zwaaf families to the OPK.

To complete the identification process, the OPK calls up 'family members' who have known my parents and me (?). Apparently, there had been publications (?) asking people looking for Jewish children in hiding to contact the OPK.

On April 9, 1946, the following persons visited the OPK offices for this purpose:
- *Mrs. Willy (Wilhelmina) van Litsenburg-Jacobs, my great-aunt, (sister of the grandmother of my father)*
- *Mrs. Duveen-Frank (a niece of my grandfather Godschalk)*
- *Mrs. Benvenida Blok-Blitz (given name Nida, niece of my father)*

Baracs shows them a recent picture of me on which I am three and a half years old. It had been sent to him by Mrs. H. Rienstra-Oosterkamp.

I believe that all the three ladies recognize in the portrait of 'unknown Gerrit' Louis Godschalk.

April 12, 1946:
Baracs writes with a pencil on an unsigned visitor's form: 'Mrs. Litsenburg (great-aunt) shows me a number of family portraits. The parable of "unknown Gerrit" with the faces of the fam. G. is indeed very big. I therefore believe I can declare that the little boy depicted on Gerrit's photo is identical with the child Louis Godschalk.'

April 26, 1946:
Baracs writes Mr. G.M. Meijer and Mr. G.F. Wiersma: 'I am pleased to inform you that unknown Gerrit, living at the Rienstra family, has been identified. His real name is Louis Godschalk, born on 1-11-1942.'

Mr. Baracs added a memorandum to his report which states that the child must be from a rich family, based on the possession of various retail premises. This means that the future of this child is now assured.

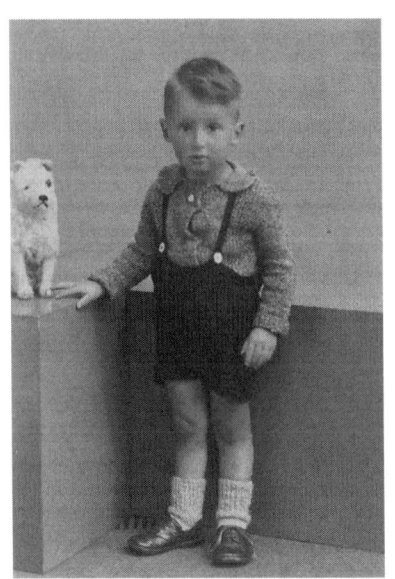

This also explains why Mr. Baracs also added to this memo that after investigating Mr. and Mrs. Rienstra-Oosterkamp in 1946, the members of the OPK concluded that the current environment in which the child was growing up did not match the standard of his original life. That he was well cared for and in safe hands, given the circumstances.

This picture was sent by Hennie Rienstra-Oosterkamp to the OPK in 1946

BEZOEKFORMULIER

BEZOEKER:
Naam: Mev. v. Litsenburg
Adres:
Datum: 12 April '46

Wenscht te spreken met: / heeft en oproep ontvangen van: H. Baracs.

Inzake OORLOGSPLEEGKIND: Louis Godschalk
(naam en voornamen voluit)

Geboortedatum(s): 1.11.1942

Dossier no. *gewijzigde and - task*

Mev. v. L. toont mij een aantal familie portretten. De gelijkenis van "onbekende Gerrit" met de gezichten van de fam. G. is inderdaad erg groot. Ik meen dan ook te mogen verklaren dat het op de foto van Gerrit afgebeelde jongetje identiek is met het kind Louis Godschalk, dat ik in Mei 1943 uit de Joodsche Crèche heb ontvoerd. —

Naar ik van Mev. v. L. vernam, is Louis vermoedelijk eenig erfgenaam van het vermogen van zijn grootvader van den zelfden naam (en grootmoeder Cornelia G. - Jacob) aanwezig: een huis v I fl 5000.- (Koopprijs 4000.-) een of meer polissen + kleinigheden. Bewindvoerder, naar Mev. v. L., is Mr Knap. Benoeming werd mij getoond (dd. 21 Nov. 1945)
Ook trouwboekje van ouders is bij Mev. v. L.

Vader: Leon G., geb. 14.7.1916 zoon v. Louis G. en Cornelia Jacob
Moeder: Anna Kwast geb. 22.9.1917 dr. v. Hartog Kw. en Clara Kwaak
Getrouwd op 5.1. 1940.

Zij vraagt het bij pleegouders te laten, indien zij geschikt zijn. Ouders waren volgens haar eigen verklaring los van het Jodendom.

Opgesteld door: (naam voluit)
Dit formulier naar Documentatie. Wordt behandeld als binnen-komende post.

Not signed visitor report of Mrs. Litsenburg

April 30, 1946:
Baracs writes the following to the Rienstra's: 'Your foster child Gerrit has been identified. His real name is Louis Godschalk. Louis was called Loekie by his parents. I am returning the picture of Gerrit, all three ladies have recognized their nephew Godschalk.'

> Nowadays, the above identification procedure would have been completely inadequate and unbelievable. This book /biography is called 'Who am I?', partly based on the situation described above.

May 14, 1946:
OPK, Baracs writes the following to the Rienstra's: *'The identification took so long because a link was missing*, please let me know as soon as possible if you have any ideas about the future of the child.'

May 26, 1946:
Feike Rienstra*answered: 'We imagine that once Loekie has completed primary school and if he is able to do so, he will go to the Higher Civic School.'

Now that the identification process has been completed, the question is who will be assigned the guardianship. The Jewish Blok-Blitz family or the Rienstra-Oosterkamp family? We must wait for the court ruling, and the recommendation of the OPK is often decisive.

June 5, 1946:
Mrs. Blok-Blitz asked the OPK for permission to visit me together with her husband Louis. The OPK, in turn, asked the Rienstra's for permission. Nida Blok-Blitz is a niece of my father. Nida and her husband received permission for the visit.

June 16, 1946:
The OPK recommends the Rienstra's to transit the guardianship application of Hennie Oosterkamp to the name of Mr. Feike Rienstra. This request was fulfilled by a letter of 16 June 1946. Hennie and Feike

decide to call me Loekie from now own, Loekie Rienstra, without any explanation. A lot of people would call me Gerrit for years to come. This sometimes led to some confusion, not least for me personally. Who am I?

June 25, 1946:
The OPK has drawn up an 8-page report. Some fragments:

Parents:
- Religion of parents: Jewish;
- Parents and grandparents from both sides were wealthy;
- *The parents had moved completely away from the Jewish religion;*
- Distant relatives and people from the neighborhood are called by name; they all declare that my parents never showed any connection with Judaism, that their chuppah* and my circumcision took place at the request of my grandparents.

Candidate foster parents (possible candidate guardian). Mr. and Mrs. Rienstra-Oosterkamp:
- Feike Rienstra*, foster father, does not read books and has little interest in the newspaper;
- Hennie Rienstra is more intelligent. Is interested in books and newspapers;
- The foster parents do not intend to let the child work as an assistant at a farm of factory after primary school, or to keep him from any opportunities to move forward;
- Naturally, Loekie is raised with the religious influence of the foster parents, although they will leave him free to decide for himself later.

Candidate foster parents (possible candidate guardian). Mr. and Mrs. Blok-Blitz:
- He has the character of a merchant, someone who likes to work hard, takes good care of his family, and cares a lot about a pleasant environment. He makes a calm impression;
- She is very present, very decisive. With great self-esteem;

- Their marriage is harmonious;
- Mr. and Mrs. Blok-Blitz and her parents are typical Jewish people.

Guardianship scheme:
- The greatest question in this case is: must Louis remain in the Dutch Orthodox Calvinistic, or move to a Jewish environment?
- Granting the guardianship to the Rienstra's seems to be justified in any case;
- Since the parents of Louis did not priorities a Jewish upbringing but rather a calm, quiet, steady development of their child;
- The interests of the child must come first;
- I do not see any reason to expose the child to the experiment of interrupting a growing bond with the Rienstra's and the potential creation of new bonds. (No name or signature)

July 17, 1946:
The Blok-Blitz couple visits the Rienstra's on a Sunday in July. After this visit, they write a letter to the OPK on July 17 which includes the following:
- We knew the Godschalk-Zwaaf family well. We, like them, grew up in a Jewish-Amsterdam environment. Lion and Anna Godschalk had not wanted their child to grow up in a Christian environment;
- They made this clear and irrefutable by the act of circumcising Louis. Undeniable proof of their wish concerning their child;
- Louis receives a Christian upbringing, which is already being enforced;
- Louis is being raised in a working-class family, in a very unhygienic environment (husband, wife and child live and cook in a room and sleep together in a small cramped attic);
- We are close relatives;
- We have the same age as his parents;
- We are of the same faith;
- We consider it our duty towards the memory of the parents, as well as the towards the child, to request you to let us adopt Louis.

July 21, 1946:
The Blok couple writes the following to the Rienstra's, among other things:
- Loekie is a striking and outspoken Jewish type, who does not fit into your environment at all;
- He will stand out from the other children in Scharnegoutum, this striking distinction will cause him much sadness as children are merciless in such cases. Loekie will never have a happy childhood in your environment;
- The parents had Loekie circumcised because they wanted him to be and remain a Jew for life.

(The Blok couple visited the Rienstra's and me again in the spring of 1956. They were not welcome. They invited me to stay with them during school holidays, but my foster father rejected the invitation. They gave me a book. Their address was on the first page. They asked me to stay in touch in writing. I remember that book. The first page is missing, torn out. It was clear who was responsible for this. My foster father saw the Blok-Blitz family as a Jewish threat).

July 25, 1946:
The OPK contacts the Main Synagogue* in Amsterdam and is informed that my parents underwent a chuppah (religious Jewish blessing of their marriage) in Amsterdam on 9 June 1940.

August 7, 1946:
Feike Rienstra also received the letter sent by the Blok couple on 17 July and writes the following to the OPK: 'We will never hold him back from the Jewish faith if he fully understands this decision. We will always leave him free in this respect.'

August 8, 1946:
The OPK writes the following to the Blok-Blitz couple: 'Confirming the acceptance of your letter of 17 July. The Commission for War Foster Children will take your wish seriously in due course.'

November 28, 1946:
Administrator Isidor Zwaaf, after the war, by the government appointed administrator for the Zwaaf family, asks the Rienstra family what proof they have that the child is indeed Louis Godschalk.

December 2, 1946:
L. Blok to the OPK. 'I take the liberty to ask you once again to pay special attention to Louis Godschalk. The child is not at the right place with his foster parents. I had hoped that the matter would be settled soon but have not heard from you since.'

December 4, 1946:
Rienstra to Zwaaf: *'We cannot prove that our boy is Louis Godschalk. The OPK informed us of this. You may be able to obtain more details from the OPK.'*

May 15, 1947:
Mr. I Zwaaf writes, in his role as administrator, to the OPK: In response to your letter of 25-10-1946. No. 100201: 'I have determined that the Blok-Blitz family still has the firm intention to ensure that Louis Godschalk will be adopted into their family.

Their motive, that the parents expressed their will regarding the way in which their child should be raised by having Louis circumcised during the occupation, is an acceptable argument.'

June 16, 1947:
The letter to I. Zwaaf signed by the OPK secretary. 'The committee decided not to change the upbringing received by Louis but to perpetuate the stay at the home of the foster parents. With all due respect for the Blok family, we believe that a transit to such a different environment would stand in the way of the further quiet development of his character and a harmonious development of his personality. Such a drastic intervention in the life of the young boy is not responsible and should be avoided.'

June 16, 1947:
The OPK secretary writes the Rienstra's: 'The handling of our petition to the District Court to appoint you as guardian will probably not take place before fall because of the many petitions that are still pending.'

September 20, 1947:
The OPK secretary to Rienstra: 'We hereby inform you that the OPK intends to submit a petition to the District Court of Amsterdam concerning the guardianship and the supervisory guardianship of your war foster child in which it appoints you as a guardian and Mr. I. Zwaaf as the supervisory guardian of the child. We request that you sign this declaration and return it to us. In due course you will receive an appeal from the court to be heard at the hearing.'

January 6, 1948:
The Jewish institution Le-Ezrath Ha-Jeled* (Helping the Child, LEH; Foundation for the care of Jewish War Foster Children) requests the District Court of Amsterdam to be granted custody over me. 'Also, on behalf of the following LEH members of the OPK, the undersigned permits himself to inform the court of the following:
- The OPK has decided to nominate Mr. Rienstra as the guardian to your court;
- The parents were members of the Dutch-Israelite Main Synagogue in Amsterdam;
- They had their son circumcised during the occupation, which means that there is no doubt that these parents wished their son to be raised in their own religion; that the boy is cared for by a Dutch Orthodox Calvinistic family and thus alienated from the Jewish faith of his parents; that this is contrary to the general principles of Dutch law. That, moreover, a family member, Mrs. Blok-Blitz and her husband, are willing and able to take this minor into their family, and to raise him in the faith of his parents.

The aforementioned members of the OPK therefore permit themselves to request your court to transit custody to the LEH/ Jewish institution Le-Ezrath Ha-Jeled.'

Mr. Reine Friedman-van der Heide.

July 22, 1948:
Free in accordance with the Law.
In the name of the Queen,
DECISION.
The District Court of Amsterdam, Sixth Chamber.
Considering the petition submitted to the District Court by the Committee for War Foster Children in Amsterdam. Whereas the Court can therefore accept the proposal of the Committee concerning the custody,
DECISION: Appoints Feike Rienstra as guardian.

The Rienstra's, now officially my foster parents, of which I was kept unaware, decided not to call me Louis Godschalk. I remained Loekie Rienstra. I discovered my own name 'by accident' on a day at the beginning of the second year of the MULO (More extensive advanced Primary Education), abbreviated MULO. But more about that later.

Processing everything, I allow myself the following comments:
- *I have a lot of doubts about all the conclusions/statements of Baracs in his role as the director of the OPK. When I often ask him if he is 100% sure that I am Louis Godschalk, which is an important and pressing question for me, he avoids the question and does not give me a direct answer. The outlined identification process reaffirms my negative feelings.*
- *According to Baracs, there were more than 2000 Jewish OPK orphans. Who of them was who, who of them was I, who am I really?*
- *The (majority of the) employees and contacts of the OPK, often involved in saving Jewish children during the war, had only one goal: to 'de-Jewish' the Jewish children. The OPK could use this information to advise the court to let these Jewish children, who had gone into hiding*

with Christian foster parents, to be adopted by these foster parents. This was the feeling I got after reading my OPK report in 1980;
- Why did the government leave this work to this resistance fighters? Courageous *people who had put their lives at risk to save me and other Jewish children during the war, but who were not specialized in this work. It revolved around the Jewish war orphans, why did the government not appoint a committee consisting of Jewish persons, specialized in these matters? Was this government, just like the government in London, not interested?*
- *Hitler wanted to kill all Jewish children. The twenty present Dutch Jews who serviced the war wished, to keep the Jewish orphans to continue to live as Jews in a Jewish environment, being he bricks for their future Jewish community. In the Netherlands before the war, every religious community took care of their own widows and orphans. The Jews in the Netherlands tried to convince the government, that only they, exclusively, had the right to take are of Jewish orphans. OPK advised the judge not to place me with my Jewish family. When I was told that I was Jewish, that was an extremely nasty burden. I was terrified to be a Jew. For years this caused a trauma with identity and loyalty problems. I ended up in a non-awakening nightmare.*
- *On May 14, 1946: OPK, Baracs writes the following to the Rienstra's: 'The identification took so long because a link was missing. This link is still missing!'*

However, there is no use trying to change the past. I personally do not agree with the decision of the OPK committee concerning its advice to the Court judge to have me adopted by my Dutch Orthodox Calvinistic foster parents, while my Jewish family with children had also submitted an adoption petition. The countries that had been affected by the war were counting their deaths. The Jews in the Netherlands were counting their survivors. The Jewish war orphans were an inseparable part of the Jewish future in The Netherlands. Growing up with Jewish foster parents, family members, in a warm Jewish environment, surrounded by children of my own age and background. This would have been possible for me. The OPK deliberately withheld this from me.

Hennie and Feike were now officially my foster parents. The OPK asked the Rienstra's for permission to allow Mrs. and Mr. Bettie and Sam Cosman* to visit me. Bettie became a nanny at my grandparents' house when my mother was born. She took care of my mother. The Cosman's, after the war, developed a positive relationship with the Rienstra's. They had a friendly and cozy relationship with each other. My foster parents allowed 'aunt Bettie' and 'uncle Max Cosman' that I stayed with them for two weeks during the summer holidays. I ended up in another world with ice cream, going out for dinner, the cinema, and the circus.

I later heard that the Cosman's had to carefully consider the sensitivities of my foster parents when it came to me. When they visited friends of them with me, or friends visited them during my stay with them, they were instructed beforehand, by my foster father, not to talk about Jewish topics, not to ask questions about the identity of their guest or make allusions to it, as their guest did not know he was Jewish. My foster father wished to keep this a secret from me. Apparently, his efforts went very far.

I stayed with my foster parents in their senior apartment in Talma State in Heeg at the start of 2004. I found a copy of the 'Bos School Atlas of the entire world in 48 maps', printed in 1952, in their bookcase. The following was written at the front of the book: '5 December 1952. To Louis Godschalk, with lots of love, from uncle and aunt Cosman.' My foster father never gave me this gift, as I was not allowed to know my real name.

I was also surprised to find the name and address of the van der Groot family from Sneek in my OPK file. I knew Louis van der Goot, he had acquired the fashion store from his parents in Sneek, shortly after Ivonne and I had opened our fashion store, the Mantelhuis, in Sneek in 1965. Louis and his wife Gerda became good friends of us. I immediately called Louis. He was as surprised as I was. We went to visit his parents in Sneek the same evening. It was a touching encounter and a reunion Louis van der Goot's parents had no longer dared to hope for. They never knew what happened to their 'Gerrit'.

Mrs. Alie van der Goot told us that she had temporarily taken care of Jewish babies during the war. She felt overwhelmed when I was brought to her. 'It would only be for a few days'. 'You were miserable and looked at me anxiously. I have lovingly cared for you for six weeks and only let you go once you had the weight appropriate for your age.'

Louis and I looked at each other. The basis for our friendship was laid earlier than we had ever imagined.

3

From warm to cold

My foster parents moved into an old house with me at the Oude Dijk in the center of Scharnegoutum. It did not become a real home. What I later learned from stories and what I felt myself when I grew older was that the atmosphere at our home was totally different from the loving atmosphere at the Oosterkamp family. I was no longer give any love or attention. When I touched or even tried to touch mama, my foster father would spring into action. He did not tolerate that mama got involved with me, gave me attention or taking care of me.

He did not tolerate that mama got involved with me and or gave me attention. He was also very strict for her. I had to strictly adhere to all kinds of house rules, rules that could change from one moment to the next. Everything felt cold at our home.

In August 1946, we moved in Scharnegoutum to the Kerkepad, next to my 'grandparents, Tjitze and Trijntje Rienstra'. A section of the Kerkepad runs parallel to the cemetery around the reformed church. 'Grandfather Tjitze Rienstra' had started a cow milking plant in Loënga, a hamlet halfway between Scharnegoutum and Sneek. It consisted of a handful of farms and day laborer cottages at the foot of a mound. There was a belfry, the imposing church with its gabled roof tower was demolished in the eighteenth century due to lack of maintenance. He had to give up his cow milking plant once he became incapacitated at a young age at the end of 1923. They had two sons, Feike (1921) and Gosse (1923).

My grandparents moved from the Kerkepad to the bridge keeper's house on the Zwette, in Scharnegoutum, in the beginning of the 1950s. Grandfather had been given a job as bridge keeper at the drawbridge over the Zwette. The milk factory stood opposite the bridge keeper's house. It was wonderful to be with them. My grandmother Trijntje greeted me every time with: 'Want to hug grandmother?' When I now hug my grandchildren, I think about 'grandmother' Trijntje. They were not rich. 'Grandmother' kept everything: things like corks, caps and silver foil so that I always had something to do crafts with. They received benefits from the Labor Council due to the incapacity of my grandfather. The diaconate of the reformed church supported them with food and coal when it was winter. During winter, 'grandmother' only lit the stove to prepare a meal in one pan around six o'clock in the evening. We could eat with them, as mama received too little household money to buy food. We would all sit around the stove with our plates on our laps. When the stove cooled down, we went to bed in our own home to make us feel less cold.

The house at the Kerkepad was as ramshackle as the previous house. It was draughty on all sides and the roof was leaking.

Did we really need to live so impoverished? Not if it was up to mama, she was used to meticulously running the household of her father. But my foster father demanded extreme frugality, despite the fact that there were and remained just the three of us, as their marriage remained childless. The benefits provided by the National Organization for Assistance to People in Hiding (LO*) also transferred to my foster father after the war once he married Hennie and took over to my care for me. In any case, my foster parents should have been able to pay for their subsistence with their income. However, his priority was not a pleasant family life.

Less than a year later, in June 1947, we moved again, this time all the way to Munnikeburen in the south-east of the province Friesland. My foster father started to work there as the second milk inspector at the local milk factory. No more visits to 'grandparents Oosterkamp and Rienstra' or other 'family members'. I did become a regular visitor of the director of the milk factory: His wife fell in love with the little boy with large, brown eyes and dark curls. I also regularly visited

Mrs. Damsma, the wife of the deputy director. There were hardly any children of my age to play with. Hennie must have felt displaced but did not complain one bit. She tolerated and endured it, just like she accepted all the unreasonableness of her husband.

Munnikeburen-Langelille did not last long. We went back to Scharnegoutum on July 25, 1948. My foster father would start as the first milk inspector at the local milk factory. This turned out well for all three of us. One of the factory houses, number 191, position on the Zwette, was available to us. Close to the house of my 'grandparents Oosterkamp', who lived at number 188.

There was also a boy of my age living in one of the factory houses, Sietse Meinsma. His slightly younger sister was called Peggy. The grandmother of mama, Eelkje Boersma, was still alive. As a toddler I had no idea that she was actually my 'great-grandmother'. I called her, to distinguish her from 'grandmother Trijntje Rienstra and grandmother Klaske Oosterkamp', 'grandmother-with-a-dead-cat', following an event that had stuck with me. Her cat had been hit by a car in front of her house.

4

What everyone knew, except me

On the one hand, I have good memories of the years spent before and after the primary school in Scharnegoutum. The mischief, the nice events on and outside the schoolyard, everything was very normal. But there were also moments where I must have been extremely insecure. There were events in which I was in the center of attention, without knowing why.

I will talk about one incident to illustrate this. My first school year started in April 1949. The first three grades were in one room with teacher Wytzes. It was strange to me that from the start she called me 'Little Jew', not Loekie. I must have asked about it often at home but was never given an answer. If I look at the class photos from that time, you can see that my appearance differed from that of my classmates,

Class photo 1949/1950. Louis: bottom row, second from the right

but you could not see these differences as a kid, let alone that I would ask questions about it.

The school year had only lasted a few weeks before teacher Wytzes entered the classroom angrily. 'Who had dared to write "teacher smells" on the schoolyard with chalk?' Naturally, we were first silent, but it did not take long before someone raised a finger, pointing in my direction with the message that 'Little Jew did it'. My classmates joined in. I was not aware of anything. Unlike now, it was not unusual to apply 'corrective measures'. I can still feel the pointer on my behind, so to speak. During lunch break, I told my mama what had happened and again when my foster father came home for dinner. My foster parents did not take this opportunity to tell me about my 'past'. But this corporal punishment went too far for my foster father, he immediately visited the head of the school, Mr. Hogeweg, and asked for an explanation that afternoon. My story was confirmed by teacher Wytzes in our presence. Mr. Hogeweg gave me pencil and paper and asked me to write down 'teacher smells'. I failed, I had not attended kindergarten. Teacher Wytzes and the headmaster will undoubtedly have been deeply ashamed.

The incident had a happy end in this way. A few days later, teacher Wytzes took me to Sneek. She bought stamps and an album for me at the Baarda bookstore. She showed me several times how to arrange the stamps in the album at her home. I enjoyed it straight away and was allowed to take the album home. I had a hobby now. This did not mean that I would be spared unjustified accusations when something happened from now on. The fact that you 'looked different' was sufficient to be 'suspicious', even then. I have trouble accepting to this day that everyone in our village knew that I was a Jew, except for me.

I had friends, of course. I played a lot with Feike Rienstra, a cousin of my foster father. We especially enjoyed playing soccer. Feike was a lot taller than I was and I felt safe when I was with him. This was also the case at his home and I have nice memories of his parents, 'aunt Aagje and uncle Brucht'.

I cannot forget Klaas Jellema, of course. He lived on a farm just outside the village, a wonderful place to play. I loved helping transfer milks to the cans. Klaas' father would give me his coveralls and clogs. I spent many carefree hours there.

At the farm of Bote Jellema, the father of my friend Klaas

Because of the frugality of my foster father, it was quite unique that I became a member of the local Excelsior music band when I was eight years old. I remember starting with a corhorn, then a bugle before moving to the trumpet, my favorite instrument. There were no financial options for things like school swimming, something that was at least as important. Besides music, I also enjoyed practicing my speaking skills and I even won prizes at Frisian recitation competitions that were organized in the village. I can still see myself standing there on stage in front of all those people.

The atmosphere at home left a lot to be desired, I took every opportunity to 'look for warmth' elsewhere. If I was not at one of the boys in my class – Peter Wiersma, Hotse Bajema, Douwe Rozendal, Joop Koopmans, Klaas Jellema, Freek Haan or Ate Jellema – I would be at one of my 'grandparents'. As a child, you apparently have an unconscious antenna for these things.

According to my foster father, I was a very poor student, at least that was what he often told me. Just like he had done when he was young, he wanted that I should go work at a farm to earn my own living. I was not sure what my plans were, but it certainly was not starting to work on a farm.

I may be getting ahead of things but of all the activities I developed later, my introduction to Max Abram (Appendix 10) was of decisive importance. As an evacuee during the war in Scharnegoutum, was hiding with the Abma family, one of the four bakers in the village. Max was called Jan Dekker and was eight years older than me. Mama later informed me that she had told Jan about hiding a Jewish baby. He dropped by to visit me every once in a while. Of course, I cannot remember this, but I met him in the fifties when he visited the Abma family. I would sometimes be invited to have lunch with them.

5
1956: The year of the truth

We now decide what form of secondary education children will go to in the eighth grade, but this used to be done in the sixth grade. This choice now depends (partly) on the exams taken throughout the school year but this was simpler in the sixties. This does not mean that it was better. The advice of the schoolmaster would be very important at the time. He thought I could go to the HBS (Higher Civic School) but could not convince my foster father. He wanted me to go to work straight away but the headmaster objected to this. They reached a compromise after a heated discussion. Instead of the HBS, I was sent to the MULO (Advanced Primary Education) in Sneek, the Rehoboth school to be precise. In hindsight, I think the main reason for this was that the schoolbooks at the MULO were free, while they needed to be bought at the HBS.

I later learned that the headmaster had written a letter to director Mr. Atema of the MULO with information about my name and my background. It was a bit unreal, my real name was Louis Godschalk instead of Loekie Rienstra, which I did not know myself, just like I had no idea of my Jewish origins. The headmaster asked the director of the MULO to inform all the teachers and the staff of the name I would listen to. This went fine during the first year. I liked this school, had good grades, and I went to the second year without any problems.

Things went wrong on the first day of the new school year 1956-1957. A new teacher had started at the school, unfortunately, I have forgotten his name. He read out our names to get to know us as quick as possible. Students had to raise their hands when his or her name was called out. He called out 'Louis Godschalk' and no hands were raised. Something did trigger inside me, as I had seen the name on letters at home. When I asked about it, my foster father told me that it was none of my business. The teacher asked again: 'Who is Louis Godschalk?'. I hesitantly raised my hand and said that I had seen that name on letters at home, that I did not know who that was, that I was Loekie Rienstra. A few classmates confirmed that this was true. The teacher thought I was making a fool of him on this first school day. He grabbed me and took me to the chamber of the director, Mr. Atema. He told his story. Mr. Atema realized that he had forgotten to inform this new teacher about 'my name', he had to resolve this issue. Before he informed the teacher, he gave me permission to go home for the rest of the day. 'We will address this next day.'

1955. The director of the MULO, Mr. Atema the right side, second row, first person. Louis second row left, third person

I went home confused and upset, told mama my story, and asked who Louis Godschalk was. She told me with tears in her eyes that I should ask heit (father in Frisian) when he came home around 12.30 o'clock for diner. A little later, I told him what had happened to me that morning. 'Oh, there must have been a mistake in the school records. Do not worry about it.' But I felt something was not right, even though I was only thirteen years old. I had noticed too often that people started whispering when I came close and I always was given evasive answers at home when I asked questions when strange things happened around me. Apparently, there was a big secret with me and about me, something I did not know. This time, and the only this time, from 1945 till 1962, when I left home, mama dared to stand up for me. She could no longer handle always being secretive and not telling me the truth. 'How often have I asked you, begged you, to finally tell Loekie the things he has the right to know. We cannot keep it a secret from him forever. If you refuse to do it, I will.' Hearing this must have confused me even more. Of course, I cannot remember this conversation verbatim, but I can still feel the silence once she finished speaking.

There was no way back for my foster father. But rather than realizing that resistance was no longer tenable and tell me the truth like a 'father', he dismissed it with a few sentences. I was a Jewish child who had come to mama and her father, two brothers and one sister. I was adopted by them after the war because my real parents and close relatives had been murdered. In my memories, this explanation was brief like that. I would not have heard it if it was any longer. The words I just wrote down already contained so much information that it must have been dizzying.

What I was told on this summer day in 1956 was so incredible that I cannot really comprehend it to this date. Your identity changes from one moment to the next: not a Frisian but a Jewish boy, a mama who was not my real mother, a father who was not my real father. How to process this as a thirteen-year-old? I could not. This resulted in immediate serious mental problems. I do not think I can say much more about this major event at the moment. I was not allowed to ask questions or to discuss it at home about the strange thigs that happened around me.

I went back to school the next day, Mr. Atema was waiting for me and took me to his chamber, where the teacher was already waiting. 'I am really sorry about what happened yesterday and that I was angry with you, I am truly really sorry.' He stood up and gave me a hand. I remained Loekie Rienstra but now knew who Louis Godschalk was. I later wondered when I would have learned about things had this incident not taken place.

All things considered, I went back into hiding but now in my own inner world with confusing thoughts. I had nobody to rely on who understood me and could give me support and answer my questions. I believe that this is the worst thing that can happen to you at that age.

I went to school but was not able to listen. I was confused. I was nervous and afraid when I would be murdered, because my Jewish family where murdered because of being Jews. When would I, a Jew, be murdered?

I was told at the end of this school year that I had to repeat it because of 'insufficient learning result's'.

6

From the village to the city

The efforts of the post-war reconstruction period started to bear fruit. Most Dutch people were doing a little better financially. That was also noticeable at our home, as we moved again in 1957. We stayed in Scharnegoutum this time. We moved to our 'own home'. The household money that had been accumulating thanks to the extreme frugality of my foster father was put into a new, detached house. Of course, this was not enough, and the rest had to be financed by the bank. By which I mean that cutting back on household expenses was not enough. Nothing changed in this respect.

The ambitions of my foster father had not yet come to an end, the moving truck entered our street again two years later to take us and our stuff to a new home. To the Dirk Boutsstraat in Leeuwarden-Huizum to be precise. He had a new job at De Friesland. The work involved daily visits to milk factories in Friesland to check the hygiene during the processing of the milk.

I went to the exam class of the MULO in Leeuwarden. I continued my 'musical career' at the Euphonia Music Corps, where I could play the trumpet, my favorite instrument. I met Lieuwe Tiemersma there. He was very musically inclined and played the saxophone in the local band 'De Mikado's'. I started, organized and became the president of Dutch Orthodox Calvinist Church youth association in Leeuwarden-Huizum. 'De Mikado's' took care of the (dance) music when we organized our regular festivities.

The shocking event described in the previous chapter and the many questions that remained were never answered. I think, or am quite sure, that I have subconsciously repressed it. The real confrontation came later. I cannot remember any negative comments or anything like that at school or outside. I think that was an advantage of living in a city.

I kept meeting regularly was Jan van der Berg. I knew him from the MULO. The unique thing was that when he later married his Channa, they together chose to become Jewish. That is and was not an easy matter. But they ultimately managed to do it. Jan changed his name to Moshe Wetberg. During the period that we had our office in Leeuwarden, Moshe regularly visited me. Moshe started working in Amsterdam at the offices of the Jewish Community in Buitenveldert, our contact continued.

As I write this down, I compare it to my own history. I was born as a Jew, raised as a Gentile, and was unpleasantly confronted with my 'being a Jew' in 1956. You cannot redo history, but I desperately wanted to.

7

On my own two feet

In 1960, I was 17 years old by then, I passed the final exam of the MULO with reasonable grades. What now? I asked myself this question long before the exams. Give into the wish of my foster father to get to work quickly, or opt for further education? I was inclined to pursue this last option as I intuitively felt that you needed a good education if you wanted to achieve something in life. My school organized an informative meeting where various education programs were presented. Of course, I attended it. The presentation of the Professional School for the Retail Trade in Groningen fascinated me. On the one hand, the program did not last too long, only two years, and on the other hand, moving to Groningen would give me the opportunity to stand on my own two feet. It was time to move away from the poor atmosphere at home. Besides these two practical arguments, the nature of the program also appealed to me. Retail, doing business, I had some ideas about that. I had already gained some experience during the time we were still living in Scharnegoutum.

I remember how Mr. Baarda of the Baarda's book shop, in 1955, asked me to sell saving stamps for him. When a card was full, people could cash it in at the store by purchasing a book or something else. 10 percent of the stamp sales would be for me.

I must say that I was quite good at this. No matter how young I was, the kick of a successful transaction felt good. Of course, I did not know that there might also have been a hereditary factor as I did not know at that time that my parents and grandparents had their own retail stores. I did know how much I enjoyed staying with uncle Sam and aunt Bettie Cosman in Amsterdam. They had a liquor store in the Albert Cuypstraat 206. With the market so close by, I heard and learned how to sell something. In short, my interest in retail did not come out of the blue.

I took the brochures home to discuss the idea. The thing I more or less already expected, happened. My foster father refused to bear the costs. He advised me I contacted my administrator, Mr. Beekhuis, appointed by the court. Mr. Beekhuis told me that the government had started to pay compensation to war victims through Jokos* and Cadsu*. This enabled me to finance my studies in Groningen myself.

1962. Sam Cosman* Albert Cuypstraat 206 Amsterdam

I rented a room near school, just like my school friend Henk Boetje, who also lived in Leeuwarden. I must say that I enjoyed what I learned. I made new friends, some of whom became very good friends. I am still in touch with Gerrie Hendriksen from Hoogeveen, as well with Lolke Baarsma from Zwaagwesteinde until his death.

I did not have in Groningen any negative experiences resulting from me being a Jew. Well, maybe one time. In the last and second year, in which I had to do a daily internship once a week After first having worked in a menswear shop, the school send me to start at C&A*. The human resources manager asked me of which Roman Catholic Church I was a member during the registration interview. I told him that I was Jewish, the human resources manager left the room to return a bit later to inform me that C&A only worked with Roman Catholic interns. This was sixteen years after the war! Research by historian Kai Bosecker shows that the board of C&A collaborated with the Nazi regime during the Second World War. Exit C&A.

The HEMA did not have this kind of anti-Jewish attitudes. I could start at the Groningen branch under the supervision of Mr. Prummel the next week. I learned a lot from him about the HEMA logistics, sales promotions and after-sale service. I was able to apply what I learned myself later into my own fashion shops business. He was a very nice, friendly and competent man. When we opened our second fashion shop in Leeuwarden, he worked at the HEMA in Leeuwarden. He was delighted and proud of my business success. We kept in touch till 1981.

8

The crucial years

I received a letter at the start of 1962 informing me that I had to go into the army in August of that year. Of course, I had heard stories about what to expect but I was not really worried about it at that time. I had proven that I could take care of myself during the two years I studied in Groningen. I liked sports, I did not shy away from the physical activities that were an important part of the militarily training. The fact that I am not very tall did not detract from that. I was quite looking forward to it, despite the fact that Ossendrecht was at the end of the world for me. It was about six hours travelling from Leeuwarden.

The group consisted of all types of persons and I did not stand out at all with my name. However, I never felt really at home in this group. I am still not sure why this was the case precisely. It may have had to do with the fact that I came 'from the province' and could not get used to the way the others, walked, talked and treated each other. Unconsciously, I was also still looking for myself.

The fact that I, was asked to study for ammunition supply supervisor in Utrecht after three months of basic training was good for my self-confidence. This program came with the rank of non-commissioned officer. During this program, I noticed that I could put into practice much of what I had learned during my studies at the Professional School for the Retail Trade in Groningen and at the HEMA. Besides knowledge of the product – ammunition – logistics was extremely important. What munition do you need at your base, how do you distribute the surplus among the other military locations, and when do you need/buy ammunition for scheduled drills? I felt like a fish in the water and benefited a lot from it when we had our own group of fashion shops.

The program had only just started when I was called to the base commander of the barracks in Utrecht. It felt like you had to go to the chamber of the Director of the MULO because of something you had done. But this could not have been further from the truth, it was a very pleasant conversation, I enjoyed a cup of coffee and a cigarette. This was still allowed in those days. The base commander asked me a lot of questions of where I came from, what studies I had followed, what my home situation was like, etc. A few days later, I was ordered to report to Major Slagter in Arnhem. I again had this 'called into the chamber feeling, which was reinforced by my fellow students this time. 'You must have talked about what we are doing here' and more scaremongering.

I went to Arnhem by train next day. I was expecting barracks or something like that at the address that was given to me but not the building I was standing in front of now. I thought I had been given the wrong address and looked further down the street. After walking back and forth, someone approached me and asked me what I was looking for. I gave him my instructions. 'You are at the right place, Major Slagter is the Rabbi* of the Jewish Community in Arnhem. The building is the synagogue*.' A synagogue? The situation became more and more confusing, I did ring the doorbell. Looking back, I think that this was one of the most important actions in the search for my past.

Somebody opened the door and I was taken to the office of Major Slagter. He was wearing a black suit, not a uniform. As I was taught, I introduced me with my name, army unit, and service number. The major quickly explains why he invited me. 'Why did you register yourself as Louis Godschalk of the Protestant faith? Godschalk is a Jewish name, and aren't you a Jew?' His tone is not accusatory but rather understanding. This direct confrontation breaks me. The tears in my eyes tell him that I am at a loss for words. There you are, a Dutch Orthodox Calvinistic educated boy from Leeuwarden, while your foster parents expect you to be baptized at the end of that year and confess before the Dutch Orthodox Calvinistic church in the presence of the whole congregation.

I tell him my history, he shows me an army list with names: Chaim Aaronson, Roman Catholic; Jacob Levy: Roman Catholic; Sam Groenteman: Protestant; Louis Godschalk: Protestant. All of Jewish birth. The Jewish community is looking for them. He had seen my name on the list with names of new conscripts. He had contacted me with the permission of the army command. Rabbi* Slagter proposed sending me to the Talmud* Torah School* in Amsterdam for one day a week, where rabbi Jitschak Mundstück would introduce me to the Jewish faith, culture and philosophy. This would be for the duration of my military service. I gladly accepted his proposal, as I felt I should not miss this opportunity to learn more about myself my past, my roots.

I have not regretted it for a moment. Rabbi Mundstück was a teacher in the best sense of the word. He found an inquisitive student in me. I bought the books I needed in Amsterdam at the Jewish bookstore Joachimstal. Bea Polak* was the owner. I had met Bea and her husband Wim a few times when I was staying with friends of them, Bettie and Sam Cosman. To recall, Bettie had been the nanny of my mother (Chapter 2). At one of these meetings, Bea had told me that she had met my mother a few times. When I entered their store, it felt familiar right away. These were people who could help me. Bea knew exactly which books I needed to master the basics of being a Jew.

I was used to going twice to church on Sundays, I wanted to experience a 'Jewish church service'. Bea and Wim had expected my question, they invited me to have the Sabbath* meal with them on Friday evening, before the beginning of the Sabbath, to be able to go to the synagogue* just before Sabbath begins. A greater contrast with what I was used to on Sundays is almost impossible. I could not yet read The Siddur (Prayer Book) with Hebrew texts that I received when I entered. I recognized a few words I had learned from Rabbi Mundstück but did not understand the context of the prayers and what was read during the service. However, I felt the emotional charge in word and gestures, the associated connectedness. I did not feel alone, I felt being a part of this group. It is not important whether you know each other by name. I experience the faith together with people I had never met before.

When I go to my synagogue nowadays, I am often a little bit earlier when nobody will be there yet. It allows me to feel close to my father and mother. I experience this closeness intensely. The service will look 'messy' to an outsider, to put it carefully. You enter when you want to, talk to the persons you like to talk. Children do not need to stay in their seats. Small children walk around, get sweets. Everyone is well aware of the essence of being together, of praying together.

Once I completed my studies in Utrecht, I was transferred to the De Wittenberg barracks, near Garderen. I was given the position of non-commissioned ammunition officer in the 930 Light Air Target Artillery division with the rank of sergeant. This was not successful. First of all, I was not given sufficient cooperation and understanding from my immediate superior, an older professional sergeant major. We did not have a connection. And as often happens in situations like this, the subordinate is the one who is blamed if something goes wrong. It may have been just me, but I noticed an anti-Jewish attitude in his comments.

There was also an error of judgement regarding my supervising when it came to difficult people. There was a group of boys from Amsterdam at the barracks. When you talked to one of them, there were no problems and they would walk through fire for you, so to speak. But once you had to deal with them as a group, they became unruly. I was registered as born in Amsterdam I was given the task of leading this group and keeping them in line. This did not work out at all. I had by far not the education, and mentality, also not experience to lead and large group of unruly naughty boys.

I started talking with the army doctor and he helped me. Once I had told him about my experiences with the sergeant major and the guys from Amsterdam, he made sure that my daily work was no longer supervised by this sergeant major and that an experienced older officer would keep an eye with me on the guys from Amsterdam. This was a relief. I should not forget to mention Herman Gelderman. This fellow non-commissioned officer ensured that the division commander, without my knowing, was kept informed of my activities. I could always visit this commander to talk with him. He gave me permission to attend the Talmud* Torah* School in Amsterdam every Thursday. When Rabbi Slagter or Rabbi Mundstück asked for extra leave of absence during Jewish Holidays, he always approved it. I was also free on Sabbath*, which I compensated by being present at the base on Sundays.

1963. Louis during military service in the Wittenberg barracks

I have called this chapter the 'crucial years'. In addition to what I have described above, I should also mention 'love'. Before I was enlisted into the army, there were plenty of opportunities to meet girls in Friesland.

But the few times a girl took me to her house to meet her parents, things did not work out. It was never stated directly but the fact that I was Jewish put an end to things. Rabbi Slagter tried to help me by bringing me into touch /organized that I was during the weekend invited by with Jewish families with a daughter of my age. Because they saw me as a Frisian boy with no knowledge of Judaism, the result was the same. I asked the rabbi to stop these invitations.

I did not go to the dance evenings that were organized at the base. I preferred to study or work on my photo hobby. The geography teacher in Groningen had taught me how I could develop photo rolls and also how to enlarge photos. With this I was able to do my fellow non-commissioned officers a favor and earn something extra.

I once attended one of these dance evenings I started talking with a nurse from the Goois Children's Hospital. I found out she was also Jewish. In order to not to mislead me, she told me she just had new boyfriend, Tom Busschbach from Bussum. To cut a long story short, Tom and I became friends, he broke up with his girlfriend and we started to hang out together. Tom told me about his neighbor Ivonne de Graeve, a very nice girl. He managed to arrange a date with her. Ivonne would take her friend Marjan with her now I could come along as well. I remember it like yesterday, it was a Sunday evening, 23 February 1964, at a dancing in Apeldoorn. Marjan was a lot taller than I. I asked Tom if I could dance with Ivonne. He did not mind. Dancing and talking with Ivonne. I instantly wished that this lovely lady would become the love of my life. At that time, I only hoped that I was dancing with a lady who would become my wife a short time later. It was love at first sight. It does exist. This feeling never passed. Now, more than fifty years later, our dance is far from over.

Dancing with Ivonne was very special. After the dance we got into conversation. To avoid a disappointment again, I cautiously asked her if my Jewish identity would be a problem for her or her parents. Ivonne started to laugh and told me that her father told her, after she had broken up with her boyfriend: 'You will meet another guy soon.

Ivonne in 1964

We do not care who', and he laughed and added, 'even if it is an old Jew.' 'As long as he is nice and takes his responsibility for you, he will be welcome here.' 'My parents will certainly not object to a *young* Jewish boy.'

The next day I made sure I could handle a number of ammunition matters near Amsterdam in the afternoon, after which I would visit Ivonne in Bussum without prior notice. Her father, Jacob, opened the door and said, 'Ivonne is not at home, she is still at work. But come on in.' Her mother, Corrie, and her two brothers Fred and Rob were in the room. Ivonne came home a bit later. 'What are you doing here?', she asked surprised. I can no longer remember my answer.

As warm as my reception with Ivonne's family was, so difficult was Ivonne's and her parents meeting with my foster parents.

My foster father directly made it clear to Ivonne that a marriage would not be in the cards if it was up to him. It had to be a girl with a Dutch Orthodox Calvinistic upbringing. This viewpoint was not uncommon in these mid-sixties. On the other hand, he should have known that the time of 'arranged marriages' was over. Mama did not stand up for me, maybe she wanted but did never tried to contradict her husband. Nothing had changed in all those years in that respect. The visit did not last long, that should be clear. Ivonne quickly realized what was up: 'Everything tells me that mama loves you a lot but that this makes your foster father jealous as he wants all her attention.'

As unpleasant as foster father's point of view may have been, I did not have to worry about anything, if I had reached the age of adulthood (21). I also decided that I did not want to continue living with my foster parents when I finished my military service.

This brings me, to conclude this chapter, to the following typical incident which was directly related to my foster father's behaviour. My birthday, November 1, 1963, I celebrated around that day with my friends at home in Leeuwarden. My foster father opened a door of the dresser which was always locked. He gave me a pair of shoeboxes as a kind of gift. It contained letters and utensils that had belonged to my family.

I left the shoeboxes for what they were, because what he told me next made me speechless. 'I made the transaction of your life a few years ago.' There was real estate in the form of two plots at the Jodenbreestraat in Amsterdam that had belonged to the parents and brothers of my mother. I had become their legal heir. Because the buildings on these plots were lost in the war, the owner (I) had a duty to rebuild them. The plots were mortgaged. A 'third party', not mentioned by name, had declared itself willing to pay off the mortgage through civil-law notary Rupp in Amsterdam to become the owner of the plots. He would also fulfil the reconstruction obligation. These parties arranged through a civil-law notary that, as I was still a child, the matter would be submitted to the subdistrict court in Sneek, which accepted the transaction based on the submitted documents. My foster father was required to sign.

I did not ask questions like: 'Why did you not refuge to sign. Why did you not write to the notary and district court that they had to wait until I was 21?' Why the hurry to sing? Why did you inform me, 'uncle Max Cosman or the administrator, Mr. Beekhuis?' I did not ask: 'What was the actual value of the plots?' because I would not have received an answer anyway. The enormous surplus value had now come into the possession of this 'helpful third party'.

9

1964: The year of the awareness

It should be clear that the lessons of Rabbi Mundstück only increased my interest in the State of Israel. I wanted to visit that country. Rabbi Mundstück opinion and advice was that I should visit Israel immediately after my military service because there was a chance that my social career would delay it. That would be the right time to go. I had not yet met Ivonne when I booked the trip. This would not have changed my decision, but it would have made me hesitate a moment. I was looking forward to visiting the country of the sabras. This nickname for native Israelis comes from the sabra cactus that grows in the country. Just like this plant defends itself with its sharp spines, an Israeli defends himself against injustice and attacks on his territory.

My 21-month military service was over on May 8, 1964. I enjoyed the time spend. I had learned a lot and gained an enormous experience. I was also glad that I had been given the opportunity to learn more about my roots. What made the scale turn towards the positive was the fact that I had met Ivonne. I had to temporarily say goodbye to her when I left for Israel by car.

I could not take the entire route by land due to hostile neighbors and had arranged that I could board a ship with my car in the port of Civitavecchia – near Rome – to take me to Haifa. I met Shmulik Shelef on board. He was returning to Israel, together with several kibbutz* friends. He and his family lived in the Na'an kibbutz. He suggested that I would visit them for a couple of weeks. There was sufficient work to be done at the kibbutz for me to earn my stay. I accepted his offer eagerly. Living and working on a kibbutz was so completely different from what I was used to in the Netherlands. A special experience. I remained in contact with Shmulik and his wife Nurit. They visited us in the Netherlands back in the summer of 1980.

I also received an address in Tel Aviv where I could stay for a few days. This is actually a bit of a sad story. I had met Mrs. Hiegentlich at the Talmud Torah School. She told me that she was about to move to Israel – go on aliyah* – to marry there.

Her future husband was a religious Jew, which is why she wanted to explore the Jewish Orthodox* way of life with the help of Rabbi Mundstück. She would really like it if I would visit them. I was glad to accept the offer. But her future husband died suddenly just before she was due to leave. She no longer had a reason for her aliyah* but the invitation was still open. Now on behalf of the daughter Mrs. Harari. She now lived in the apartment of her father with her husband and child. I stayed there for a few days, Mrs Harari introduced me to the Walzer family, who lived in the same flat. Their son Ami was of my age and served in the army. He was home during the weekends and acted as a guide to introduce me to Tel Aviv and its surroundings. This is the fastest way to get to know a country and its inhabitants.

It might be good to tell something about the situation of Israel in 1964. Its population was already over 2 million. In 1948, when the state of Israel was founded, this was less than 800,000. Achieving this growth in such a short period of time required great motivation and perseverance. The dream of founding and maintaining an own state is to date still the strength of this country. Despite the constant enemy threat from the surrounding countries.

Shortly before returning to the Netherlands, I visited Nes Ammin, an international Christian working and living community near Akko. Nes Ammim means 'sign for the people'. It is based on the principle of the connection between Christians and Jews. The project is committed to meetings and dialogues between Christians, Jews and Arab Israelis. Nes Ammim is set up as a moshav (a cooperative agricultural settlement in Israel) and has a number of things in common with a kibbutz*. When I told the pastor of the Dutch Orthodox Calvinist Church in Leeuwarden about my planned Israel trip, he gave me an information brochure about Nes Ammin.

I went home full of impressions with the conviction that this was not my last visit. And it certainly was not. Ivonne and I would go back as often as we could. As Rabbi Nachman of Bratslav (1772-1810) once said: 'For 2000 years, Jews everywhere remained faithful to their vision of Zion and held fast to their link with it. Wherever I go I am going to Israel.'

Back to Italy by boat. Ivonne had received permission from her parents to fly to Rome so we could go back home together by car. That is exactly what happened but not before we got engaged in the Lido-di-Roma with the intention of getting married at the end of the year.

It was time to report to Max Abram. I had looked around during my military service and had talked with De Bijenkorf and the HEMA in Amsterdam. I wanted to work in or near Amsterdam. I was offered positions at both companies but did not accept them. The wages were less than half of what I received as a sergeant. I was not really demanding but I thought I could do better. And that turned out to be true. All these years, I had kept in touch with Max Abram, who had

gone into hiding in Scharnegoutum just like me. He later started working for his father, who had a wholesale business in women's and men's clothing in the Albert Cuypstraat in Amsterdam. I regularly visited Max and his father when staying with the Cosman family, who had their shop also in the Albert Cuypstraat.

Mr. Max Abram

Max Abram had started his own business. Clothing company Max Abram. Max also opened his first ladies fashion stores under the 'Mantelhuis' Because I had the necessary diplomas and certificates, he suggested that I come work for him. Max could use my papers for a new 'Mantelhuis'. In addition to a fixed salary, I would share in the profits of the shop. This sounded interesting to me. I started working on August 8, 1964.

My work: Max bought mantle fabrics. When lady coats had to be made, I made sure that all necessary materials: fabrics, lining, shoulder pads, buttons, etc. would be ready and delivered to workplaces who worked for Clothing Company Max Abram. I also helped with sorting when large batches of ready-made products were purchased and needed to be delivered to the stores in Hilversum, Rotterdam, and The Hague, or sold to retail shops. I was introduced to the clothing trade in a short period of time, including the art of selling.

I was lucky when trying to find a place to live. As someone who just started working, you should not hope to rent a house. At that time there already was a housing shortage. Luckily, I knew Dago and Anneke Boas. I knew Dago from my military service. He and Anneke married after Dago's military service. They could move to the apartment of his parents in Amsterdam.

They had a room left for me which could barely fit a bed. But that was enough for me at that time, a bed and breakfast. I would have diner and spend the evenings at Ivonne in Bussum anyway. There was one drawback; the cooperation with my colleagues was far from optimal. I had a leadership position during my service, there people had to listen to me. This was no longer the case. Mr. Abram had talked to my colleagues after I raised the issue with him, but this did not help.

Something happened at the start of October of that year that brought my unprocessed past to the surface. I was driving through Amsterdam to do shopping for lining, shoulder pads, etc. when I suddenly felt unwell and stopped in the middle of the road. A driving instructor stopped behind me. He immediately called the Municipal Health Service when I failed to provide a clear answer. Luckily, everything ended well as far as the material side is concerned. I told my general physician I visited the day after about my anxiety, fears about my Jewish identity, and my problems at work. He asked me if I can explain this anxiety and I told him about the start of my life as I know it. Maybe the following event can make this clear.

I visited the house where I was born at Réaumurstraat 22 with my aunt Bettie Cosman at the start of 1961. The façade reads 'De Verfton'. I pondered the idea of continuing the business of my parents once I leave military service. A first glance is enough to put this idea from my mind. No maintenance had been carried out since 1943 and the building was now uninhabitable. It was rented by Mr. Joffer. He told me that his father found out in 1949 that the owner (me) was living in Friesland. That was all, there had been no attempts to get in touch with me. Joffer jr. bought the building from me in 1964 and sold it again. The new owner converted it into a house. We visited one of the neighbors. She neighbor told me: 'Your parents went into hiding after you were born. When there was a risk of a house search or raid, you were hidden in a closet. Sometimes you were brought to us around the back of the house. But you were not always safe here either. One time, two German soldiers suddenly entered the room.' 'What is that child doing here?' 'Oh, he belongs to my daughter', I answered as neutrally as possible. 'She went out to the city. Do you want something to drink? The men refused and left.' This event and others described above are a tremendous detriment to the sense of security that is essential for children. (There is now a name for it, PTSD: post-traumatic stress disorder.) The general physician prescribed a couple of days rest after hearing my story. I later told acquaintances the name of the general physician, they told me he had been a collaborationist during the war. I wonder how he must have felt during my conversation with him. I started thinking, and discussed with Ivonne, about the possibility could solve the problems at work by opening a fashion shop myself. After all, did I not have the papers for it?

There was no time for rest, I repressed this incident, as Ivonne and I were getting married! The day was November 5, 1964 and our marriage took place at the town hall in Bussum. It was a beautiful day with the parents and brothers of Ivonne, Ivonne her family, my foster parents and the brothers and sisters of mama. Most of the other family members came from Ivonne. My aunt Willy was there too, unfortunately the Cosman's were missing. Aunt Bettie had died a few years earlier and uncle Sam had passed away in the spring of 1964. My great-cousin Nida Block-Blitz and her husband Louis would certainly have come but had emigrated to Australia in 1961. We had already celebrated with my Frisian friends in Leeuwarden. I was so proud of 'my bride'. Ivonne looked radiant and I was visibly amazed.

Our wedding picture in 1964

Living space was already scarce that that time, especially in Amsterdam. Ivonne would remain with her employer Transmark until the end of the year 1964 and stayed with her parents for that time. I might have been able to stay with Dago and Anneke for a while, but this would not solve the problem of having our own place. We bought an 18-meter long houseboat at the Da Costa quay. We put sing: 'Beit Sjelanoe', our house. Now we owned our dream palace with a mezuzah* on the front door and all interior doors. Ivonne started working for an insurance company in Amsterdam on January 1, 1965 and our 'own life' could start. Doing things together and making decisions together, a new world opened up for me. I was no longer alone with my emotions and could share them with Ivonne.

When moving into the houseboat, I looked at the shoe boxes my foster father had given me on my 21st birthday and which I had left untouched until then. Apparently, I had not been ready to confront my past. I placed the two silver Shabbat candlesticks, the silver teaspoon, the sugar caster, the cake server, the copper spoons, two golden rings, the silver ring with the initials LG, and the golden pocket watch on the table in front of me. They had all been possessions of my parents. I felt their proximity when I imagine how they were used and worn by them. This is what I still have of them and it will not become more. I will need to accept this. I later placed the pocket watch in a glass jar and gave it a place of honor in my office to remind me of the fact that my past will always stay with me.

I regularly encountered the name S. Baracs on letters with an address and telephone number in Amsterdam. I looked the phone book and find the same address and phone number for the Baracs name. This could not be a coincidence and I dialed the number. Mr. Baracs himself answered and when I told him who I was and why I am calling, I heard him shout: 'Hester, I have Louis Godschalk on the line, one of your missing babies!' Mrs. Baracs answered but had trouble speaking as she tears up. We agreed that we would visit them the same evening. They welcomed Ivonne and me like welcoming their own children who they had not seen in a long time. The Jewish Council* appointed Mr. Walter

Süskind as Director of the Hollandsche Schouwburg. Mr. Walter Süskind, managed to persuade my parents to let the Trouw resistance group working from the nursery opposite the theater get me to safety. Hester van Lennep, now his wife, told me how they did this. I was taken from my bed in the nursery and wrapped in a blanket. I was brought to the Hervormde Kweekschool (the Protestant Teachers College) in the Plantage Middenlaan through the garden in the back.

She took me to her home address on the Keizersgracht by tram or bike. Someone from the Amsterdam Student Group made sure that I was taken to a safe address. She had lost track of me at that point. She was overjoyed that I had come back to her. It is also remarkable that the students of the Protestant Teachers College saw what happened but that no one betrayed it.

I indicated back in Chapter 2 that I seriously question the veracity of the statements above.

I regret not opening the box sooner as it also contained a list of names of family members who survived the war.

Mrs. Wilhelmina van Litsenburg-Jacobs, Mrs. Duveen Frank, Benita Block-Blitz, Johanna Godschalk, Ester Jacobs, Isidore Zwaaf, Catharine Zwaaf, Joseph Zwaaf, W. Zwaaf, Mrs. Mimi Agsteribbe-Zwaaf, Hans-Wouter Hartmann jr., Mrs. L. Zwaaf-Stoete, Mrs. Jetje Gerritse-Aldewereld, Mrs. Rachel (Chelly) Zwaaf-Aldewereld, Marianne Westerveld-Aldewereld, Heintje Mulder-Aldewereld, Schoontje Groen-Aldewereld.

In 1965 I did not have the strength to start to try to contact my living family. Only in 1980, after reading my OPK file got the courage to do. Much too late. I only managed to contact a few of them in 1980, the others had already passed away.

It may seem like my life on the Amsterdam canal had calmed down, but this was not actually the case. Mr. Abram told me at the end of

1964 that the agreement about 'a store using my own papers' could not go through. The same agreement had been made with a colleague, but he had made too many mistakes when carrying it out, which had cost Mr. Abram a lot of time to resolve and he did not want to take that risk again. It is was not a sign that he did not trust me, as became clear a few months later.

Because the relationship with my colleagues failed to improve, Ivonne and I decided, after lengthy discussions, to start our own fashion store. I had started to become familiar with the particularities of the job and Mr. Abram turned out to be an enthusiastic and committed supporter. If we wanted, we could make use of his 'Mantelhuis' name and use the advertisements of this 'brand'. Ivonne was regularly invited to join someone from the head offices to become acquainted with the job of fashion store manager. Mr. Abram only had only one condition: 'Not in my backyard.' He was planning to open a lot more 'Mantelhuis' stores. We accepted the proposal and quickly found a location as far as possible from Amsterdam: Sneek! The sales territory of this city is large and had sufficient potential for a fashion shop. Everything was

1965. Louis in front the display window of 't Mantelhuis
for mother and daughter in Sneek

gaining momentum. Ivonne quit her job, the houseboat was sold, and we rented a shop with upstairs an apartment in Sneek at Oosterdijk 18, with the agreement that I had the right to purchase the building after 10 years at the price fixed in 1965. Mayor Rasterhoff opened ''t Mantelhuis Godschalk' on August 27, 1965.

Ivonne was in charge of the daily management with Mrs. Klaas de Boer as first assistant. The coats were provided on consignment by Clothing company Max Abram during the first period. Later, when we had 'saved up', we also visited other suppliers to purchase products. I was back in Sneek and things had changed a lot! The city itself was mostly the same but I had certainly changed. I had left as a child and had come back as an entrepreneur! There was not much time to think about this, the store was (fortunately) a success, also thanks to the parents of Ivonne who helped out in a lot of ways. Mama helped as well, and she came to the store from Leeuwarden whenever she could. You could tell that she loved it. She did more laughing working store in one afternoon, than a year at home.

Success demands more. We opened the second location in Leeuwarden at Nieuwestad 70 on March 11, 1967 with the same purchase condition as in Sneek. Another year later, August 22, 1968 to be precise, the third shop opened, this time in Groningen at Herestraat 70. It may be faith, but we became the neighbors of C&A, the same branch that had refused me an internship when I was studying in Groningen because I was not a Roman Catholic. In the end, we opened a total of seven shops with the head offices and distribution center in Leeuwarden.

Because Ivonne and I were constantly on the move and we needed to make sure that the stores were supplied and operated in the way we wanted, there was not enough time for another important aspect: accounting. I took the overly impulsive decision to ask my foster father to take on this task. He was almost fifty. He had been having for long time issues at work. People of his age already had difficulties finding another job. He had taken an accounting course. Rationally speaking, one plus one makes two, but I was wrong. Foster father could not get used to the fact that he was now subordinate to his foster son. He was used to always making decisions for the other persons around him but this time it was the other way around. He made decisions where he did not understand the consequences. He sent and signed, without my knowledge, large and incorrect bank payments to the bank. Despite our agreement that he would only deal with the controle of the shops administration, he began to arrange all kinds of things, all beyond his (bookkeeping) duties. This escalated so much that I had to ask him to look for another job if he really was unable to change. Foster father believed he did nothing wrong and suggested that the minister of his church should mediate. If he was right, nothing would change, if I were right, he would be willing to look for another job immediately.

He was shocked when the reverend did not agree with any of his arguments. I suppose that the minister has had, after this first meeting many conversations with him. When foster father could not find another job, a situation became acceptable. From then on, he slowly started do only did his own work. It speaks for itself that the mood at the office improved vastly. One less thing to worry about.

Our daughter Anna Vanessa was born on December 15, 1969. It was a fantastic experience to give life to a next generation. Of course, all parents have this same thought, but it was very special in relation to my parents I did not get the change to know.

I will leap four years ahead. It is now 1973 and we have moved to Tietjerk, around 10 kilometers east of Leeuwarden. We had been planning a move for a while but felt like it was unfair towards the father of Ivonne. He had spent so much time and energy on the apartment in Sneek and to leave quickly went too far for us. Our son Lion Patrick was born in Tietjerk on November 25, 1973. I remember it like it was yesterday. It was a car-free Sunday. The assistant of the doctor felt like it was necessary for Ivonne to give birth in the hospital in Leeuwarden. Ivonne refused to be transported in his old Citroën 2CV. We followed him in our own car and hoped that we would not be stopped by the police. The trip and the delivery went well and there would be four of us from now on.

Ivonne did not feel at home in Tietjerk and told this to a neighbour. Unexpected I received a call at some point with the question whether we wanted to sell the house. It was not a complete surprise. We quickly agreed on the price. Our next home was in Stiens, around six kilometers north of Leeuwarden, where my foster parents lived as well. Ivonne no longer needed to hurry to be home when the children came back from school as mama was always willing to act as a babysitter. Anna Vanessa and Lion Patrick could also sleep there if this was necessary. We lived in a former farmhouse with a pond in our front yard. This is where the kids learned to ice skate.

Was it not time for us to take some rest? Yes, but in my own way. We purchased a weekend house at the waterfront in Idskenhuizen, halfway between Sneek and Lemmer. We would entertain ourselves on or near the water from Friday afternoon to Monday morning. There was no time to really unwind, as I now realize. Moreover, after 'nine years of women's fashion', we had the feeling that the market was changing. Our advertising agency carried out a market survey. We discussed it with Mr. Seesing, our business advisor and bank director, together with our buyer/stylist Ineke de Groot. Our feeling had been right, and the stores were restyled into trendy boutiques in the same year, 1974. They served a younger generation with different requirements. Mantelhuis Godschalk became Lilou (Lion and Louis). Together with our professional fashion buyer/stylist Ineke de Groot, I visited all fashion centers in Europe to get acquainted with the newest developments and to make the corresponding purchases. We also purchased in the Confection Centrum in Amsterdam, now called World Fashion Centre. Kolbo 2001 was also located there. I had already met Simon Meerschwam (Appendix 12). I would later do business with his son.

Materially, we lacked nothing. Still, it dawned on me in the mid-seventies that this could not be all there is. Did I need to demonstrate that you can return from an almost hopeless situation to a socially

1974. Opening of Lilou Amersfoort, our seventh shop.
Ivonne is the second from the right

successful career? Not at all. My father role triggered my trauma of being a Jewish child in hiding. I lived between a lost and a new generation. Having my own children was a victory over evil. The chain of my family, from generation to generation (Le Dor Va Dor*, appendix 2) had finally been restored and became even stronger when I became a grandfather.

10

'What does it mean for us to be Jewish?'

Our work and family absorbed Ivonne and me completely and the exploration of my Jewish identity was pushed into the background. I do not use this as an excuse but rather to indicate that apparently I was still not able to fully confront my situation and subconsciously preferred to stay 'in hiding'. A number of events contributed to the fact that I was forced to face the truth.

Starting in 1967, Ivonne and I regularly visited Israel, which was always a pleasant reunion with friends I had made in 1964. This was also the case in 1974, when we visited the Fashion Week in Tel Aviv. An office of the Jewish National Fund (JNF*) was located opposite our hotel. One of the activities organized by the JNF was a 'tree planting day'. You purchased a tree and could plant it yourself at a location indicated by the JNF. We decide to use this great initiative to plant a tree in memory of my murdered parents. The driver of the taxi asked for whom we had planted a tree when returning to our hotel.

I briefly told him that Ivonne and I had planted a tree in honour of my murdered parents. That I was saved during the war by a Christian family. The driver asked us if we knew that the State of Israel honours these 'saviours' and has even established a special government institution for them, Yad Vashem, the World Holocaust Remembrance Centre, on the western slope of Mount Herzl, also known as the Mount of Remembrance, in western Jerusalem, Israel (Appendix 6). The 'Avenue of the Righteous among the Nations' is part of this memorial in memory of the thousands of Gentiles who had risked their lives to save Jews during the Holocaust. These 'saviours' are honoured by the right to plant a tree in the Avenue of the Righteous among the Nations. If they had died, this right transfers to their children.

Ivonne and I looked at each other and we knew who we were both thinking of, mama and her father. The JNF provided me with the necessary forms and conditions. This award would only be granted after careful research. It required witnesses, for example. Correspondence to Yad Vashem had to be send trough to the Israeli Embassy in The Hague. All in all, it took years before a decision was taken. It would take until 1981 but more about this later.

I was given the first warning that something was wrong with me back in October 1964, when I literally and figuratively lost my way. The general practitioner in Amsterdam only advised me to rest a few days. I did what he recommended and did not pay any more attention to it and it was not strange that it repeated itself two years later. I visited the general practitioner in Sneek, who admitted me to the hospital. Examinations did not yield any results and I was sent home after a few days. This returned in an intensified form in 1976, I fell into a deep psychological crisis with everything that goes with it: terrifying dreams, waking up screaming and covered in sweat. I was sure that it was not because of the work, as it was my passion. My work was playing the main role in my own film. But what was it? Memories from my earliest childhood that I had not processed yet? The consequences are not difficult to guess. I became tired, functioned poorly, and became aggressive. Back then, I was already choosing to go along with my delusions rather than to seek help.

'Grandpa Bussum', as our children called the father of Ivonne, died in 1977. We would have loved to have kept him with us for so a lot longer as we loved him a lot. He was always a good father-in-law for me, from the first moment we met him. He was interested in everything I did. The same was true the other way around but I would quickly lose track once he started to talk about technology, particularly when it related to cars. I only knew how to start my car.

The question Anna Vanessa asked one day in 1979 when she came back from school seemed simple: 'What does it mean that we are Jewish?' She was asked this question by the father of her girlfriend, who was the headmaster of the primary school in Stiens. I had to prevent that I am being a Jew for her, personally at school, for her not would cause unpleasant consequences.

I did not want her, suddenly, to have an identity and loyalty conflict. The fears of being a Jew and the nightmares I had experienced myself, I had to prevent that this would happen to Anna Vanessa. A flashback threw me back to 1956, when I came home with the question 'Who is Louis Godschalk?' This had thrown my whole life into a black hole and this should not happen to our children. I cannot remember my 'provisional' answer. I do know that Ivonne and I decided to actually give substance to my Jewish identity together with our children. This was a choice for a new beginning with all the consequences arising from living in accordance with the Jewish tradition. The ultimate question that comes with this is 'who am I?' Part of the answer lies in the past, with my ancestors through my parents. They had succeeded in keeping the connection with the Jewish past. The line that connected me with this had become very thin.

It was already fifteen years ago that I had received lessons at the Talmud Torah school in Amsterdam during my military service. It was time to get back to it. There was a small Jewish community in Leeuwarden and I became a member of its synagogue.

Mr. Ewald Cohen, chairman of the board, took me under his wing and Ivonne joined us a short while later. The strength of the Jewish tradition lies in 'remembering and preserving' (shamor and zagor). A lot of attention was paid to this in the lessons.

Mr. Cohen invited us to his home so that Ivonne could meet his wife and daughters. They explained to Ivonne what it means to run a kosher* Jewish household as part of the kashrut*. One of the consequences was that our kitchen had to be completely redecorated for this – the fastest thing was to buy almost everything new - was soon clear to us. Ivonne was the driving force in this kind of practical things. Ivonne tried to create a Jewish atmosphere at home, especially on Shabbat.

Our children were automatically taken along in this change. You could say that this slowly answered the question raised by Anna Vanessa in practice. When they became adults themselves, they decided to also become Jewish (to come out) by meeting the requirements that make a transition to Orthodox Judaism possible. In Judaism, parents pass the values and traditions on to their children. Parents do not only prepare their children for the future but also introduce them to the past, the historical chain of 4000 years of traditions.

Thanks to Ivonne, I was able to pass on the 'torch of the Jewish tradition' of my murdered Jewish family to our children, who in turn pass it on to our grandchildren Shiraz, Ron, Ady, Idor and Iron. From generation to generation ('Le Dor Va Dor'*) (Appendix 2).

Ben Gurion was right when he said: 'A man who does not believe in miracles is not a realist.'

Naturally, this change had an impact on our business activities. We decided in October 1979, to try to sell a few shops to free up time for me to study Judaism. We talked to Mr. Rijkens, a real estate advisor in Amsterdam, and presented our plans to him by the end of October 1979. He saw opportunities and we gave him until the end of January 1980 to sell all or parts of Godschalk B.V.

I went horseback riding with Anna Vanessa one Wednesday afternoon in November 21, 1979. I had promised it a long time ago. Anna Vanessa asked me to fulfil this promise. After riding a few laps inside the horse ring school, I had a blackout and fell from the horse and became unconscious. When I woke up, I discovered that I had broken my left wrist. My long and short memory was gone. My ability to remember things never completely recovered after. It was good that Mr. Rijkens succeeded in finding a buyer for Godschalk B.V. We signed the deeds at a civil-law notary on January 31, 1980. I used some of the proceeds to buy three retail properties, two in Sneek and one in Drachten. I rented these out to others. It took a lot of effort, but the day came on Monday March 30, 1981. The Yad Vashem ceremony for Hendrika Rienstra-

Oosterkamp and her father Klaas Oosterkamp (posthumously). We had offered my foster parents a group trip through Israel without informing them of the real reason. The trip was organized by the Friesch Dagblad. The tour leader, Mrs. Van de Wetering, was aware of

1981. Planting a tree in Yad Vashem
First row: Ivonne, Anna Vanessa and Lion Patrick.
Second row: foster father, Louis and my foster mother

the true purpose. Ivonne, our children Anna Vanessa and Lion Patrick and I flew to Israel a few days in advance.

My foster parents were very surprised when they saw us. They were even more surprised, mama cried when we told her what would happen the next day. We had invited our Israeli friends. The Dutch ambassador to Israel, Mr. Verkade, also attended the ceremony with his wife and daughters. Mama planted a tree, also on behalf of her father, at the Avenue of the Righteous on the Mount of Remembrance in Jerusalem. The tree has a plaque with their names. Mama received the Yad Vashem medal and the Yad Vashem certificate during the ceremony at the Yad Vashem center. I held a brief speech.

I felt that a period in my life had ended and that I was ready to enter the next phase when this highest honor by the State of Israel was granted to the lady who not only opened the door of her father's house during the war but also her heart.

Plaque at the tree

11

The new life

Our daily lives had undergone a profound change. No longer leaving early and getting home late to ensure that all shops, head office and distribution center would continue to operate optimally. What remained were the activities that had to do with the rental of the purchased buildings and settling the sale of Godschalk B.V. I could largely arrange these from my writing desk at home. Nothing stood in the way of moving, not within the Netherlands but across the border. Ivonne and I discussed this.

America was an option as friends of us had gone there, friends went to Florida and others to Los Angeles. We had no idea what to expect there. We did not want to take this step without preparing. You must at least spend a couple of months there to see if the country, the culture, and the population suit you. There were too many uncertainties and it would distract me from my new direction I had taken into my life. We decided we should not be looking to the west but to the east, to Israel to be precise. The first steps had already been taken with the regular visits to the country and a recent one-month Ivrit 'training course' at the Ulpan* Akiva in Netanya. People with different nationalities are taught the basic knowledge of Ivrit. (modern Hebrew)

Ivonne and I felt that trying to give our children a Jewish upbringing would best be done in Israel. In 1981, it was almost forty years ago that I was born a Jewish boy. The umbilical cord that connected me to the Jewish traditions was cut after only eight months. Ivonne and I wanted to repair this connection. Inadvertently, I think of the text of 'Whither Thou Goest', sung by Leonard Cohen. The song is about Ruth, a lady who decides to become Jewish. Her husband has died, she is alone with her Jewish mother-in-law Naomi, when she says: 'For wherever you go, I will go. Wherever you live, I will live. Your people will become my people, and your G'd will become my G'd.' (Ruth 1:16) She marries Boaz in Bethlehem and becomes the matriarch of King David.'

I discovered the same determination to want to belong to that people in myself. In other words, I was ready to go on aliyah. Ivonne did not need convincing, she fully supported me, as she had always done. The transition could be difficult for the children, we were well aware of that. We tried to tell them what to expect as well as possible. The departure would be difficult for the mother of Ivonne and my foster parents.

I still needed to find someone who could take care of the remaining businesses, including the rental of the properties we owned. This was impossible from Israel, especially in that time. Communicating with the Netherlands by telephone was cumbersome because we only got our own telephone connection in 1986. The fax only started a couple of years to gain popularity and the Internet was not known at that time. Mail was especially dramatic, and it could easily take a few months for a letter to arrive.

I had met Koos Boorsma when arranging the mortgages for the new bought buildings in Sneek and Drachten. In 1980 Koos worked at the financial services center Eerste Friese'77 in Leeuwarden and lived in Britsum, near us. The way he arranged business matters related to mortgages gave me confidence that I could ask him to look after my businesses. He accepted after a meeting in which I told him what I expected from him. This partnership lasts to this day to the satisfaction of us both. It is clear that the business relationship has turned into a friendship after 37 years. He also played an important role in the realization of my biography by putting my 'story' on paper in a way that fully does justice to my own ideas. I will always remain grateful to him for this.

We left the Netherlands on September 7, 1981 and were housed in a shelter in Ra'anana when we arrived in Israel. Our shaliach Zvi Nadav – representative of the State of Israel in the Benelux – had advised us to do so as it made the next step easier. Mirjam and Zvi Nadav lived in Ra'anana. They were always willing to asset us. We had three rooms at our disposal and that was fine for the time being. The school for the children was nearby and Ivonne and I could go to the ulpan* for our learning Ivrit. People from different Israeli ministries came by to inform us and help us on our way at set times.

We stayed there for half a year, after which we moved into an apartment nearby in Ra'anana in April 1982. This meant that Anna Vanessa and Lion Patrick could stay at the same school. News spreads quickly in small communities. This was also the case for our arrival. Of course, you quickly meet your neighbors, but we did not expect to meet a namesake. We had been living there for a few weeks when the doorbell rang. The lady on our doormat introduced herself with a big smile as Sara Godschalk. She had heard that a namesake had moved to Ra'anana and wanted to meet him. Of course, she also wanted to find out if we were family. We call this sorting out of family relationships 'doing mishpokhe'. This turned out not to be the case, no matter how far back in time we went. She and he deceased husband had already moved to Israel from Zwolle in 1936. Her youngest daughter Regina lived with her husband Chaim next to her in Ra'anana and her other two children, Aviva and Jitschak, lived in kibbutz Urim. They were always very hospitable, and we could always rely on them. When we had questions. We were always invited to celebrate with them all Jewish Holidays or other festive events with them. This is how we integrated into Israeli life.

While children can playfully master a new language, this was more difficult for Ivonne and me. Of course, we went to the ulpan* but it remained a laborious process for me. I was happy to meet Rabbi Nathan Dasberg as he spoke Dutch. He was the director of the Kfar Batja orphanage, near Ra'anana. This home and others like it were founded after the Second World War for Shoah orphans who had survived the war. He was the guide who continued helped me find my way in Judaism. I visited him a couple of times per week and went with him to the synagogue for afternoon prayers. I do not wish to withhold a special event from you. At one-point, ritual objects were brought into the synagogue of Kfar Batja. Nothing special in itself, were it not that I heard that the sender was the synagogue of Leeuwarden, which in turn had received them from the synagogue of Sneek. The synagogue of Sneek could not be restored after the war because there were not enough Jewish residents. They were a Hanukah* candlestick and the veil of the Ark of the Covenant. The 'Lamp for the Eternal Light' should have been included but was left in the hall of the synagogue in Leeuwarden. The synagogue in Sneek had been located near our store/home in Sneek before it was destroyed during the war. I remember that a memorial stone in the shape of the Star of David was placed at the site in 1972 with the following text in Hebrew: 'In memoriam' and underneath it in Dutch: 'The Synagogue stood her until MCMXLV'. This memorial stone was placed on a pedestal in 1984. Our past had followed us, as it were.

The choice to raise our children in a Jewish environment proved to be a successful. All the more so because I had not had a Jewish upbringing myself. Our children, Anna Vanessa and Lion Patrick came into contact with the Jewish culture and its traditions in a natural way. Education is and was an important part of this as it is rooted in this society. This early period was not easy for them, but we never really heard them complain. Although Anna Vanessa enjoyed school more than Lion Patrick. We had hoped back then but we know for sure now, they are proud of the fact that they are Israelis and live in a country that is 'theirs'.

No present without a past may sound like an open door but this is the daily reality for every Israeli. Preserving your identity is nowhere as important in Israel. An identity that has its origins in the ancient dream of returning to your native country which became a reality again after about 2000 years. The people of Israel will not allow this to be taken from them. They have fought for it and will continue to do so.

I conceived the plan of becoming a guide focused specifically on Dutch or English-speaking tourists. The training was given in Tel Aviv and I completed it in 1985 to become a qualified tourist guide. I greatly enjoyed this work for one year, especially for groups with Frisian participants. I can still see their surprised faces when I responded in Frisian. Mrs. Noor van de Wetering was a tourleader on one of the trips. This was a very special reunion as this had also been the tourleader on the journey my foster parents had made where mama and her father had received the Yad Vashem award in Yad Vashem in Jerusalem.

1986. Louis working as a tour guide

Because Lion Patrick turned 13 on November 25, he became Bar Mitzvah* during a festive event on the 11th of December in the conservative synagogue of Ra'anana. His Bar Mitzvah Parashat was Toledot. The ceremony was concluded with a ceremony at the West Wall of the Temple in Jerusalem. The boys who became Bar mitzvah in that week could read a section from the Torah*. It was a moment of pride for us to see our son standing there. It was even more special for me because it made the past-present-future bond even stronger. The fact that Ivonne her mother and my foster parents could also be there, just like the Blok-Blitz family from Australia and our friends Jan and Jo Kooi*, made it even greater.

Before Lion Patrick could have a Bar Mitzvah ceremony in the synagogue, Ivonne, Anna Vanessa and Lion Patrick took an oral exam based on the requirements of the conservative Beth Din* (court) in Jerusalem at the end of October 1986. They had been taught at home for a year by Rabbi Dov Vogel. The chuppah (wedding ceremony) between Osnat Bat Ya'cov (Ivonne) and Ben Zion Ben Arjeh (Louis)

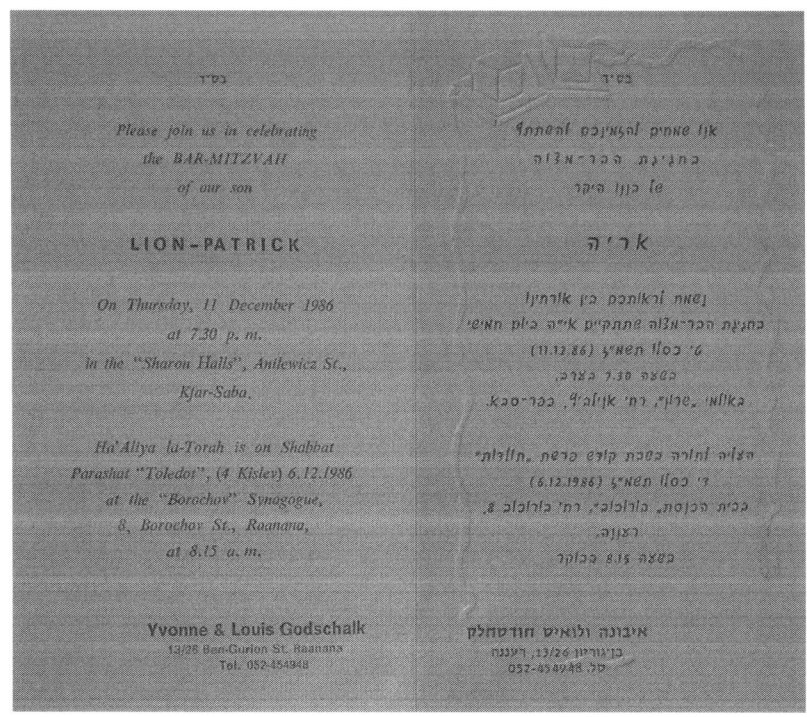

12-11-1986. Bar Mitzvah Invitation of Lion Patrick

took place immediately after the examination. We received a marriage certificate (ketubah*) of this ceremony.

I was called up for military service for the second time in my life, now in Israel. The fact that I was still a Dutch citizen could not avoid this. I knew that in advance. I do not think I need to mention that there is quite a difference with military service in the Netherlands. Just take the constant external threat. A drill could become reality at any moment. My Israeli service period as a reservist lasted from 1986 to 1994. First I had to go to a camp near Ramallah for a six-week basic training. This camp came into our possession after the Six Days War of 1967, it used to be a Jordanian army base before that. I can still feel the cold that came in through the broken windows. After this period, I would be regularly called up for retraining for periods of one month.

I suffered from an inguinal hernia in 1987 during a military service period. Nothing special in itself, if the doctors had not been on strike at that time. The surgical procedure had to be postponed a few times because of this. Finally, I contacted Dr. Brozin, who was a member of our synagogue. Although he was not allowed to operate me, I had to be operated in a military hospital. Dr. Brozin, performed the surgery, because after a couple month I only could walk with a lot of pain. I am still grateful to him.

It was also for some time impossible to walk without pain after the operation. This is one reason why I stopped working as a tour guide. My drive to tell and show people as much as possible would sometimes get in the way. I would fail to realize that participants also wanted to relax at a market or an outdoor café. The responses I would receive afterwards did tell me that people enjoyed themselves nevertheless. The fact that I had trouble walking was one reason to stop but there was also something else going on. I noticed that the issues with my memory, which started after my aforementioned fall from the horse, became worse instead of better.

I was introduced to the Rotary Club in Ra'anana through Anna Vanessa. One of their projects was an exchange program with a group of European children. This group included two children from the Netherlands but the couple where these two children stayed had trouble communicating with them because of the language. Maybe Anna Vanessa could help? She was now 16 years old, she made a good impression. Things progressed from there and I was asked to become a Rotary member. I missed most of what was being said at the weekly meetings at first because I did not understand the language very well. This went a lot better later and I have even been the treasurer of the Sharon-Herzliya Rotary Club twice and chairman once.

We had moved in 1988. The reason was material. After seven years the lack of an air conditioner became very noticeable in Ra'anana. When we first moved to Israel, our wish list was not very long. But once you experience air conditioning in friend's apartment, a few times, you realize that it is not an unnecessary luxury. The owner of the apartment did everything to install this device but failed to do so. Too many issues and an insufficient electricity grid. Moving was the only option. We found a house for sale in Herzliya. This city is built against the south side of Ra'anana, as it were. The apartment was located on the top floors of the Bar Kochba complex. You had a magnificent view of the surroundings and saw the beautifully landscaped courtyards when you looked down. The interior was in good hands with Ivonne and she turned it into a tasteful home with her skills. We had something we owned ourselves and looking back, I can say that this has been a very good period of our life.

A new highlight took place in April 1989. Mama was invited by Yad Vashem to come to Jerusalem to become an Honorary Citizen of the State of Israel. She was the fourth person to receive this honor. The first one was the Swedish diplomat Raoul Wallenberg. It was a special and moving ceremony. With her as mama, mother-in-law, grandmother and great-grandmother, we also honor her father, brother and sisters, because together they enabled me to survive during and after the war.

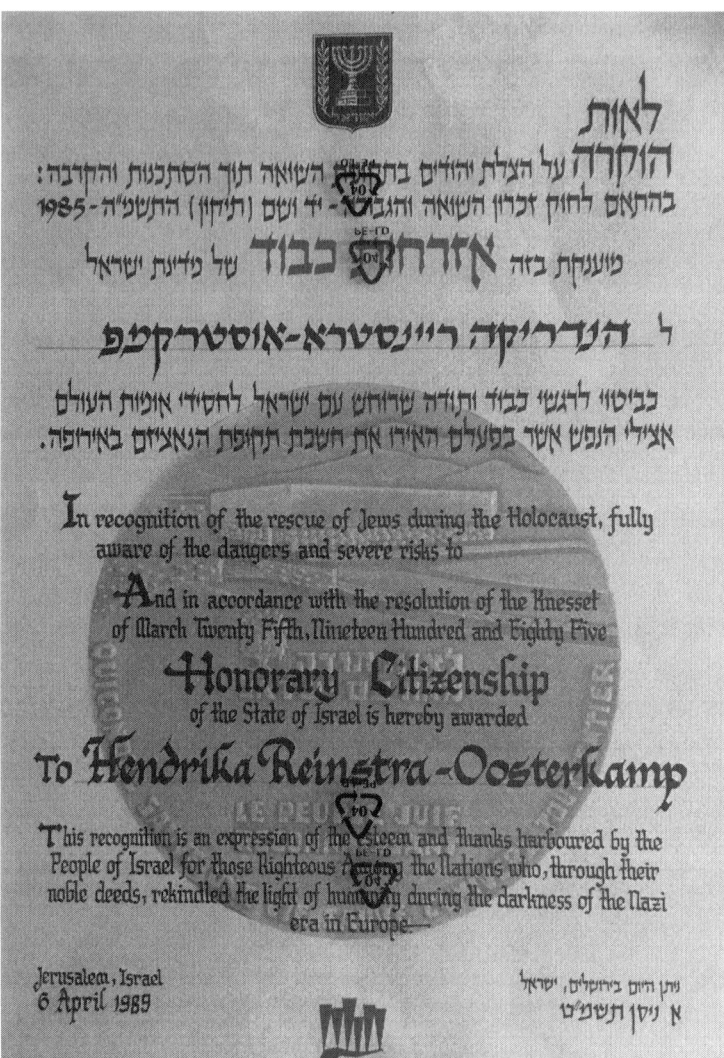

April 6, 1989. Hendrika Rienstra-Oosterkamp.
Honorary Citizen of the State of Israel

12

You are not alone

It took more than 45 years before the realization set in that a group of Jewish children had grown up separated from their parents during and after the Second World War*. These forgotten Jewish children remained in hiding in the society that had taken them in. People had failed to recognize that this separation had often caused irreparable psychological damage. As the years went by, they often became parents themselves and the need began to arise to meet each other to share their issues and experiences. Apparently, there was no room for this within the 'normal' society where people looked away from it. Partly because there were no clear answers and often because it was considered a form of ingratitude to those who had saved them. Even though this was not the case at all.

Following 'The Hidden Children Movement' which was founded in New York in 1991, a conference on 'Hidden Children was held at the RAI in Amsterdam from August 23-25, 1992. The initiators were the ICODO and JMW* Foundations. The first acronym stands for Informatie- en Coördinaticorgaan Dienstverlening Oorlogsgetroffenen (Information and Coordination Body for War Victims) and the second for Joods Maatschappelijk Werk (Jewish Social Work)*. The goal was to give a voice to those who were still young during the war. Until that time, discussions about the Shoah were dominated by those who were adults during this period.

I flew to Amsterdam to attend this 'Hidden Children conference'. The conference was opened by the mayor of Amsterdam, Mr. Ed van Thijn, who had also been a hidden child. 'We scored low on the list of Shoah experiences', he said, to indicate that little attention had been paid to these hidden children. And: 'We should be glad and did not or hardly discussed it until now.'

It was a unique experience to be with about five hundred 'peers'. I had met other people who had gone into hiding but, strangely enough, we did not discuss that specific topic. One of them was Ids Boot*, we had gone to the MULO in Sneek together. I met him here as well. Jacques Grishaver (Appendix 11), now the chairman of the Dutch Auschwitz Committee, also participated in this conference. I knew him from the period during which I went to the synagogue in Amsterdam and would meet him often afterwards.

Because age plays such an important role, the working groups were divided by year of birth. Your experience and the ability to process it depend strongly on whether you were two or twelve years old at the time. Jetty Leffring* was in my working group, both of us were born in November 1942. Jettie hid with the Wiersma family in Joure during the war. She stayed there after the liberation.

The discussions held in the working groups concerned topics we recognized to a greater or lesser extent. To mention a few:
- How do you combine affection for your foster parents and their children with the grief over your murdered family?
- What has growing up in another culture done to our emotional life?
- Why do I show compulsive behavior?
- Did we not do our partners a disservice because they were not aware of our psychological problems when they married us?
- Why do I tend to perfectionism?
- Where was G'd? How could the Beneficent allow the destruction of His chosen people?

The leaders of the working groups gave everyone the space to tell their story. Each story had the full attention of the group, so many recognizable things were told. First carefully, later with more emotions without anyone being embarrassed about this.

Subjects/questions everyone could agree on were:
- Why did we have to remain 'grateful' at all times and could we never be angry? What did this do to us?
- The anger, because apparently, I had to be ashamed being a Jew.
- Why being a Jew, does that evoke aggression in others?

Questions that did not have clear-cut answers but that had to be asked. Looking for or pointing out the guilty parties is meaningless because you would be doing what others are doing to you. It will not make you feel any safer either.

They tried to explain to us that you must stop being a victim if you want to discover your own identity. 'Because we are not guilty!' is what they kept telling us. You can only create space to develop yourself if you keep that in mind.

Mrs. Drs. Bloeme Evers-Emden summed it up nicely when she concluded her conference lecture as follows: 'We are no longer victims, we overcame, even if we did not win.'

Besides processing these difficult topics, there was also time for singing and dancing. Beautiful Jewish music was performed. Our partners were also present on the last day to get a taste of the atmosphere. This would not be the only conference, it is organized annually somewhere. A lot of things I had repressed for fifty years came to the surface. It will take a long time before the puzzle is finally put together. I am working on this to this day. Louise-Marie de France once said, freely translated: 'Suffering passes. Having suffered never does.'

13

Chasing trails

'Have you been helped or saved during the Second World War in the Netherlands by people you want to meet again? Contact: KRO television, 'Spoorloos' c/o Willy Werkman, correspondent in Tel Aviv.'

This text caught my eye when I read The Jerusalem Post of May 27, 1994. The KRO was working on a television program as part of 'The Netherlands - 50 years liberated'. I decided to respond because I may discover more about my parents, other family members, and the people who saved me, whose names appear in my OPK file. Maybe I could learn more about the ambiguous first six-month period in this file.

I told something about myself and the things I know about my family in my letter, I received a response from Mr. P.J. Vertegaal, editor of the program, on June 30, 1994. 'One of our editors, Mrs. Trudy Cornelis, will contact you by telephone soon. The creators of the program need to know what questions you have'. I replied immediately with the following questions:
- Who knew my parents, grandparents and/or other family members and can tell me something about them?
- My OPK file contains the names of the resistance fighters who were involved in my rescue. I was unable to find these people myself, maybe 'Spoorloos' can help?

Mrs. Cornelis called me for some more information. Soon after, I received a message that I am one of the four people who are invited to participate in the live TV program. The others were Ya'cov Yannay, Mirjam Wartman, and Max van Mentz/Menat.

The first recordings were made at the homes of the participants one week after the invitation. The following weeks, they were broadcast on television as informative clips in the hope that they would receive a response. Reporter Dirk Bolt stated during these broadcasts that they did receive responses, without going into the details.

We had purchased a pied-à-terre in Amsterdam-Buitenveldert in 1993. This was because of the regular visits to my foster parents and to maintain my business contacts. This came in handy now.

A few days before the program, the 'candidates' and the Spoorloos team met in Hilversum. We met each other for dinner in a relaxed atmosphere and were informed about how the program would go. We did not need to be nervous because everything was arranged down to the last detail. I was tense but mostly in the hope that I would get answers to my questions.

Mirjam Wartman was fourteen years old when the war broke out and had stayed in hiding at 22 addresses, she wanted to know with whom. Max van Mentz/Menat was looking for the people living at the addresses he was taken to. The story of Ya'cov Yannay was moving. He was looking for a German camp doctor. An exchange took place between a group of 222 Dutch Jews in Bergen-Belsen and a group of Germans living in Palestine in July 1944. The Germans considered this enemy territory. The Dutch were allowed to go to Palestine, the Germans to Germany. Ya'cov and his parents were part of the group but Ya'cov was too sick to go along. The camp doctor listened to the praying and pleading of his mother and did give permission. The trip by train through devastated Germany, Austria, Bulgaria, Turkey and Lebanon was extremely precarious, especially because of the danger of shelling by English planes. Miraculously, nobody succumbed on the way. They all reached Palestine unharmed.

The (live) broadcast takes place on November 7, 1994. Ivonne had flown in from Israel to support me mentally and because she 'wanted to be there'. I was glad that my foster parents were there as well, just

like Ivonne her brother Rob, his wife Tonny and Sjoukje and Koos Boorsma. During the broadcast it became clear that there were also guests who had responded to the TV informative clips. Debby Petter, the presenter, at one point said: 'Louis, we have a surprise for you.' At that moment Mrs. Suusje Palte-Lazeron walked into the studio. She was carrying three books and handed them over to me after a warm welcome. These are Jewish religious books that my parents had given to her father for safekeeping in November 1942. I was moved to tears and speechless, unexpectedly I received Jewish synodical books, once owned by my parents. The books have the following titles:
- De vijf boeken van Mozes (The five books of Moses)
  writer: S.I. Mulder.
- De Republyk der Hebreeën (The Republic of the Hebrews)
  writer: Petrus Cunaeus.
- Gebeden der Israëlieten (Prayers of Israelites)
  writer: G.I. Polak.

Another family member had come to the studio, Barend Zwaaf*. He could explain to me in great detail what the family relationships on the side of my mother had looked like. A few years later, he took me to the places where my family members had lived in Amsterdam before they were arrested and deported. I did not learn anything about the Godschalk side. Mirjam and Max also received the information they needed to move on. The doctor Ya'cov was looking for turned out to have died.

Debby Petter ended the broadcast with a quote from the letter of Ya'cov Yannay, one of the guests of the evening: 'Anyone who saves a life, saves a new generation.'

After the broadcast, I received a list of the names and telephone numbers of people who had responded before and during the broadcast so that I could contact them. I did so every time I stayed in Amsterdam. They were old friends from school or from military service, people which I had done business. I also visited and wrote down the stories of the children of our former neighbors from the Réaumurstraat, people who had lived in or in the neighborhood of the Réaumurstraat, who had taken the trouble to respond. A daughter of one of the neighbors of my parents could confirm the story I had heard from her mother. She confirmed that I was placed in the linen closet or brought to her parents when another search was expected.

Mr. J.G. Schellings had also called with the message that he still had old telephone books of Amsterdam. After calling him, he sent copies from the, General Address Book of the City of Amsterdam', 86th edition, 1939-1940 (Address Book), containing the names, addresses and telephone numbers of the families Godschalk and Zwaaf. When I compared it to the Jewish Council* (Registration List), combined with the information of the people who knew them, the picture became clearer.

- My father Lion was born on July 14, 1916, my mother Anna Zwaaf on September 22, 1917; both in Amsterdam.
  The Address Book lists the following for the name of my father: 'Drogisterijen. Réaumurstraat 22. Tel. 55598 – Ringdijk 9. Tel. 55894.' My mother took care of the housekeeping and worked in the company. This was not an officially registered profession at the time.
- The Registration Lists mentions the following for my father, Lion: 'Bread supply employee. Previous job: architectural broker.' Once Jewish property was expropriated, the owners simply had to find out how to make a living. The Jewish Council did everything in its power to help them. Delivering broad remained allowed, as long as it was solely to Jews.
- My grandfather, Louis Godschalk, was born on August 5, 1888, his wife Cornelia Godschalk-Jacobs on March 15, 1891; both in Amsterdam.
- The Address Book lists the following for the name of my grandfather: Louis Godschalk & Zn., drugstore, paints, window glass, household items, contractor of painting, Molukkenstraat 138. This is where they lived at first, as their address in 1940 was Réaumurstraat 22.

At the start of September of that year, they moved to Middenweg 3 hs, with a paint supplies store at Ringdijk 11.
- The Registration List mentions the following below his name: 'Bread supply, formerly supplies'.

When my parents, Lion and Anna married, they first lived at Bredeweg no. 37, before moving to the house and store of his parents at Réamurstraat 22. Louis Godschalk & Zn. had a thriving family business which was established on May 1, 1934. Everything father and son had created was expropriated and destroyed in a short period of time.

My parents and the grandparents of my father were transported from the Hollandsche Schouwburg to transit camp Westerbork on July 7, 1943, on to Sobibor* on the 20th of that month, where they were gassed immediately, after arrival, three days later.

- My grandparents from my mother's side, Hartog Zwaaf, born on 20 October 1885 in Amsterdam, and Clara Zwaaf-Zwaaf, born on April 19, 1884 in Breda.
- The Address Book lists the following behind their name: 'Colonial goods etc.' Their last address was Jodenbreestraat 31, where they ran a business, and another one at no. 33, tel. 48372.

They were deported from the Westerbork transit camp on October 23, 1942 and gassed, after arrival, three days later in Auschwitz*.

Every time I see the copies of the Address Book, I feel the urge to dial the numbers or visit the addresses and say: 'It is me...'

Shalom my dear father,
Shalom my dear mother,
Shalom dear grandparents on my father's side,
Shalom dear grandparents on my mother's side,
Shalom all other family members who have been murdered.
I never knew you, you knew me.

I visited Mrs. Suusje Palte-Lazeron (1929) and her husband Henk Palte in Katwijk on November 16, 1994. This was in response to her surprising contribution to the TV broadcast. She had a lot to tell me, as she had waited for this moment for a long time. I think I should let her speak for herself.

'We lived at Celsiusstraat 16, near the house at Réaumurstraat 22 where your grandparents and later your parents lived. My father worked in the public garden service during the war. In his spare time, he carried out work for your parents and my mother did housework for your mother. Because your parents lived in the Jewish tradition, the store would close on Friday afternoon at the start of the Sabbath and remain closed until the Sabbath was over. My father had a key to the store so that he could help people who had forgotten to buy something during the week. My parents would also turn on and off the lights at your home and keep the stove burning during Sabbath. Your father would also carry out small repairs at other people, such as replacing glass windows. My father would usually take care of these jobs.'

I often visited my mother when she was working at your house. One day, I entered the kitchen and find our mothers crying. I asked what happened and heard that your sister had inhaled smoke and suffocated. You were born a while later. My father had attended your circumcision ceremony. He rented a black hat, black jacket and black tie for this. My mother was waiting for me at school in the Summer of 1943. She told me: 'You can no longer visit Anna. The store door has been sealed.'

Before your parents went into hiding, they gave us a wedding picture, two savings books, and three Jewish religious books. They wrote a letter from Westerbork which concluded with 'See you soon'. After the war, my father contacted the OPK and was invited to come by. He handed over the items your parents had brought to us in January 1946. Except for the three books. When he came home, he was still angry about the way he was treated there. 'The 'OPK man' had asked him all kinds of things, even about private affairs of the family. Things that were none of his business.' At the end, he was asked to sign the minutes of the conversation. When my father reads them, they contain things he had not said. He does not trust it and feels like the OPK man hates Jews. He regrets handing over the items and certainly does not intend bringing the three books there as well.

He learned that the son of Anna and Lion was still alive and that he can give the books to him when he visits the home of his parents. This is why he asked the Joffer family, who now rents in the 'Verfton', to send you to him when you visit them. (*When aunt Bettie Cosman and I visited in 1961, Joffer did not say anything to me. LG*)

My father has kept waiting for you. He became ill and died in 1993. My mother had to promise him not to throw away the books but to keep them for you. She does so but dies shorty after as well. My sister Riek and I decide that she will take the books with her to her home in Amsterdam. My husband Henk and I are watching television on November 7. I hear the name Godschalk and say to Henk: 'Could this be about Anna and Lion's baby? You know, the one my father talked about every now and then, the boy of the Jewish books.' Henk checks Teletext and reads your call for information. I call Spoorloos, as Riek is ill. A cab is sent to Riek straight away to pick up the books and bring them to the studio. They also send a cab to me and I barely have time to get changed as Spoorloos TV was life, therefore I had to hurry. I manage this and sometime later I hear Debbie Petter say: 'Louis, we have a surprise for you.'

I am given the other items kept by the Palte family from my foster father on my 21st birthday. The letter of February 22, 1952 from civil-law notary Spier shows that they are already in the possession of my foster father. He received them from my great-aunt Willy van Litsenburg-Jacobs many years earlier. This letter did not state how these items came into her possession.

Het NIW (New Israelite Weekly) published the following on November 18, 1994: 'The television program Spoorloos invited survivors of the Shoah looking for people who are important to them for two weeks in a row. A child who was in hiding at that time was looking for information about his Jewish parents. The Committee for War Foster Children decided to leave him with his Christian foster parents after the liberation. He only discovered he was Jewish when was a teenager. Spoorloos gave him the information – stories, pictures – he was desperately looking for.'

Mrs. Henriette Boas wrote an article about 'Spoorloos' in December 1994. 'Very touching was the history of Louis Godschalk, who was placed with a family in Friesland who raised them as their own child and adopted him when his parents did not return from the deportation. He only learned that he was a child of Jewish parents as a teenager. However, he knew nothing about his family and all his attempts to look for his family, friends, or acquaintances of his parents were unsuccessful. Spoorloos managed to find a cousin of his mother and a number of children of neighbors who lived next to his parents who remembered them well.' 'Spoorloos' deserves praise for the thorough and very time-consuming research and the entire program was well put together.

I wholeheartedly endorse this.

14

The incomprehensible reality of Auschwitz

There was hardly any interest for what had happened to the Jews in the first years after the war. Those who had survived the extermination camps ran into a wall of incomprehension. They needed to support each other. However, they had to organize themselves to gain recognition. But it was not until 1956 before the Dutch Auschwitz Committee (Dutch: NAC) was founded. This committee managed to become the mouthpiece of all Jews to garner attention for what happened to them during the war years. Various activities are still being organized under the 'Nooit meer Auschwitz' ('Never again Auschwitz') motto.

One of these is the (annual) trip to Poland in which Ivonne and I took part in 1999, together with almost a hundred others from both the war and the post-war generations. Very special were the participation of Mr. Jules Schelvis, the sole survivor of the 14th transport to the Sobibor extermination camp, and Leni Boeken-Velleman, a survivor of Auschwitz. The NAC had organized it. It had delegated the board members Jacques Grishaver and his wife Loes Glasius, and Joop Waterman with his wife Judith van Geens, for this purpose. On behalf of the NIOD, prof. dr. Hans Blom with his wife Ansje Neuteboom participated, and Mr. Ronald Leopold* represented the Pension and Benefit Council (Dutch: PUR). Dr. Wertheim went along as a physician. Rabbi Sonny Herman (1927-2009) and his wife Leny ten Cate took care of the religious aspects.

So many participants, so many stories, so many expectations. The participants were a bit uncomfortable at first, but a feeling of connectedness arose automatically when we listened to each other. Whoever we were or whatever we did, we had one common denominator: Paying tribute to our parents, grandparents, brothers, sisters, and all other family members who we often had not or only hardly known. We do this at the places where they were murdered, the extermination camps. These are also confrontation camps for us as their next of kin. Facing the history of your own past, which cruelty you feel every day.

We flew from Amsterdam to Warsaw and then took a bus to the largest of all German extermination camps, Auschwitz.

It is part of the town of Oswiecim in southern Poland. About 1.3 million people were deported here by cattle wagons of which about 1.1 million were murdered, usually gassed. This is in stark contrast to the text above the gate through which they entered: 'Arbeit macht frei'. I tense up as I enter Auschwitz-I through the same gate in 1999. Although everything is a bit touristy, they managed to keep everything as it looked in the war years. A model shows the structure of the camp. The 30 residential blocks were built in 3 rows. The entire camp was surrounded with a wall with 13 km of barbed wire on top and watchtowers at the corners. A number of these blocks have now been converted into museums. There is a Dutch pavilion in which Jewish life in the Netherlands over the last three centuries is shown. The Israeli pavilion gives an idea of Judaism through the ages. This is where we lit candles and where people read out the names of his or her murdered parents or other family members. We then said kaddish (Appendix 5). You feel struck when walking along the wall against which people were shot and the inner tension was almost unbearable when entering the gas chamber. Images and more images flashed through my mind. My family was no longer treated like people here.

We then visited Auschwitz II, three kilometers away, in the village of Birkenau. If you ask someone who has not been there himself what he thinks Auschwitz looks like, he would usually describe Auschwitz II. Most Jews were kept in this enormous extermination camp. Anne Frank was also taken here in September 1944, together with her mother Edith and sister Margot. She and her sister were later taken to Bergen-Belsen, where they were murdered in February 1945. Leni Boeken-Velleman spoke the following poignant words: 'All the women from my barracks waited here for more than twelve hours to be gassed. Ultimately, we only wanted to be dead.'

The prisoners of Auschwitz I and II were liberated by Soviet troops on January 27, 1945. The Germans had fled and left behind an immense amount of goods they had taken from the prisoners. Ida Vos wrote a poem about it in 'Thirty-five tears':

> *Thousand glasses*
> *Thousand shoes*
> *Thousand wigs*
> *The world ends in Auschwitz.*

So many things were taken away, so few people were left. Only a few hundred starving people, more dead than alive. The others, including 60,000 Dutch Jews, were murdered by execution, gassing, medical experiments, or forced labor. Including relatives of mine:

On October 26, 1942:	my maternal grandfather, Hartog Zwaaf, born on 20-10-1885;
	my grandmother Clara Zwaaf-Zwaaf, born on 29-04-1885;
On October 31, 1944:	uncle Levi Zwaaf;
On October 8, 1942:	his wife Rachel-Zwaaf-Aldewereld;
	their son Hartog;

'They will never be forgotten', spoke Rabbi Sonny Herman.

Our trip continues, the cup is not empty yet. We arrive in Majdanek, in the east of Poland, near the city of Lublin. It served as a concentration and extermination camp from July 1941 to July 1944. First for Russian soldiers and from the end of 1942 also for Jews. Research shows that at least 78,000 people were murdered here, 59,000 of whom where Jews. Numbers, numbers, incredibly large numbers. The gas chamber is still there, you walk inside and try to imagine what you would feel if you could not walk out whenever you want. It is impossible to imagine. A mausoleum has been built as a memorial for the ashes of the deceased.

But the hardest part is still to come, to the northeast of Lublin. It was an extermination camp from April 1942 to November 1943. Nineteen transports with a total of 34,313 Dutch Jews arrived from the Westerbork transit camp from March to the end of July 1943. This after a horrible train journey in cattle wagons lasting three days. To reassure them, they saw 'To the sauna' or 'To the library' signs when the exited the train. I wonder what was left of this reassurance when they were ordered to undress, after which they were shaven and brought to the shower room. Their gassed bodies were brought to ovens that were specifically designed for this purpose to be burned. The following family members of mine were forced to take this journey:

On July 23, 1943:	my father Lion Godschalk, born 14-07-1916;
	my mother Anna Godschalk-Zwaaf, born 22-09-1917;
	my grandfather Louis Godschalk, born 05-08-1881;
	my grandmother Cornelia Godschalk-Jacobs, born 15-01-1918;
On May 21, 1943:	my aunt Hendrika Godschalk, born 02-03-1914;
	her son, my nephew Louis Godschalk, born 05-09-1940;
On November 30, 1943:	my uncle Simon Zwaaf, born 10-06-1910;
On May 14, 1943:	his wife Esther Zwaaf-van Beem, born 12-10-1913;
	their daughter Clara, born 01-02-1936;
On May 23, 1943:	my aunt Lena Zwaaf, born 17-03-1925;

We held a memorial ceremony at the 'Hill of the Holy Ashes'. We lit candles for the family members who were murdered here and called out their names. Rabbi Sonny Herman recited the El Malé Rachamiem prayer* (Remember). He sang-spoke it at a specific melody, which was as moving as its content:

> 'G'd full of love and compassion, whose presence is always with us,
> Grant all souls of the six million Jews, victims of the Nazi massacre,
> perfect rest under the wings of Thy mercy,

among the saints and the pure who shine in the infinity of Your being.
They were murdered, murdered as martyrs,
by the German executioners and their accomplices of other nationalities,
in Auschwitz…
Bergen Belsen…
Buchenwald…
Dachau…
Majdanek…
Mauthausen…
Natzweiler…
Neuengamme…
Ravensbruck…
Sachsenhausen…
Sobibor…
Theresienstadt…
Treblinka…,
and the other extermination camps in Europe.

Rabbi Sonny Herman preceded in praying for the rest of their souls. We mourn their passing at this place and in our daily lives; we mourn our family, loved ones, friends, acquaintances, and even the strangers who have no relatives to remember and commemorate them. Protect them, origin of all love and mercy, under the protection of Your wings forever. Bind their souls in the bundle of eternal life.

The Eternal One is their inheritance and yet always keeps justice in His memory. Let their souls rest in peace where their remains are. They have not been forgotten. And they will never be forgotten.'

Yizkor for the victims of the Shoah. May G'd remember the good:
- The souls of our six million brothers and sisters, men, women, and children, who were murdered during the Shoah in the countries of Europe during the Second World War; among them more than one hundred thousand Dutch Jews who were murdered;
- The righteous among the people who gave their lives in their lives in the service of G'd by resisting the oppressors. As we keep their

memory close in our hearts and pray for the rest of their souls, may their souls be absorbed in the bundle of eternal life, in Your protective presence, together with the souls of our ancestors and all the righteous who enjoy eternal peace, and may we always remain united with them in love. Amen*.

We then said the kaddish prayer together with the rabbi.

As I am writing this down, it sounds like cold list of facts, but nothing could be further from the truth. I experienced and remembered each moment intensely. I would process it later. When I walked around the hill a few times, I felt close to my parents and relatives. I had finally met them. Ivonne and Mrs. Judith Waterman were waiting for me, they gave me an arm, and we walked back to the bus together.

The cobblestone I was allowed to place at the Memorial Avenue of Sobibor, with the names of my family members who were murdered in Sobibor

15

These are the names

Even in the new millennium, much attention continues to be paid to the persecution of Jews during the Second World War. Rather than declining, as people intentionally thought, the flow of publications, documentaries and the like only grew. New facts come to light, witnesses of war crimes that have been silent for a long time are now telling their story. Mass graves are being uncovered and trials are being held against camp executioners. Recent memorials record the incredibly gruesome history for our ancestors in a contemporary and moving way. During the restoration and repair work in the extermination camps, the conservation teams find gold coins, watches, pocket knives, jewelry and the like that were not buried but hidden.

On January 27, 2005, it will be 60 years since Auschwitz was liberated. Auschwitz is also a symbol for all the other camps where a total of six million Jews were murdered, including 102,992 from the Netherlands. To commemorate this, the 'Westerbork Memorial Centre' and the Dutch Auschwitz Committee organized a unique project. The names of all murdered Jews and 245 Sinti and Roma are read out during a continuous period of 116 hours.

From the publication: 'On Saturday January 22, 2005 at 19:30, Dirk Mulder, Director of Camp Westerbork, Joel Cahan, Director of the Jewish Museum and Jacques Grishaver, Chairman of the Dutch Auschwitz Committee, will begin.' The last names will sound over the transition camp Westerkamp at around 11:00. These will be read by the State Secretary of the Ministry of Health, Welfare and Sport (VWS), Clémence Ross-Van Dorp, and Fia Polak, who was saved in Auschwitz on this day back in 1945.

Before the reading starts, a memorial service will be held in the Hollandsche Schouwburg. The Mayor of Amsterdam, Job Cohen, will speak there, and Rabbi Sonny Herman will say the Kaddish prayer. The participants will then walk to the Resistance Museum, during which the first names will be read out by Jeroen Krabbé and Marga van Praag. Besides the name, the family name and date of birth will also be mentioned. The 700 readers include a lot of camp and hiding survivors, survivors of those who were murdered, the ambassador and staff of the Israeli embassy, primary and secondary school pupils, city councilors, representatives of governments and related organizations, and many other people who want to show their respect. Maarten Peters concludes the project with the specifically composed song 'Names'.

The reading of the names is also expressly intended to be followed on the spot. Everyone is welcome, both in Amsterdam and Westerbork. Facilities have been placed at both locations so that the readers can be seen and heard day and night. The names will be projected on a large screen. The media will pay full attention to this project with live broadcasts, background programs and news items. NOS-Actueel will be dedicated to the manifestations in the Netherlands that take place on January 27, the date on which Auschwitz was liberated.'

All victims will be remembered in this way, one by one. The names are called out because they lived among us, a memory that will never fade.

In October 2005, the Sobibor Foundation gave me the opportunity to place a cobblestone at the Memorial Avenue, built by the Sobibor Foundation. The stone has a nameplate with the names of my relatives who were murdered there:

In memory of:

> My mother Anna Godschalk born Zwaaf
> 1917 Amsterdam – 1943 Sobibor

My father Lion Godschalk
1916 Amsterdam – 1943 Sobibor

My grandfather Louis Godschalk
1888 Amsterdam – 1943 Sobibor

My grandmother Cornelia Godschalk born Jacobs
1881 Amsterdam – 1943 Sobibor

And in memory of all the other members
of the Godschalk and Zwaaf family who are not mentioned here
by name and were murdered by the Nazis and their collaborationists

May your souls be bound in the bond of life

Louis Godschalk
2005/ 5765

I was given the opportunity to place a folder in the memorial center with a picture of my parents and the details of all my family members who were murdered in Sobibor and Auschwitz. They belonged to the group of 34,000 Jews who were transported there from the Netherlands between May and October 1943. A total of 175,000 Jews were murdered here.

The parents of Ellen van der Spiegel Cohen, a friend of ours, were the same age as my parents. Her parents were also gassed in Sobibor. She writes: 'May is the month in which the Second World War is commemorated for a lot of people. For me, it is April. Besides the joy of spring, I feel a sense of bitterness each year. My parents – barely thirty years – were both deported from the Westerbork transit camp to Sobibor on April 20, 1943. When I enjoy the white and pink blossoms in the spring sun, I always wonder if they had also seen the flowering trees from the cattle cars.'

'I weep for flowers with broken buds'.
I have always carried something of their grief and pain with me.
It will be almost April again, spring again.

I wrote this poem last year:

APRIL, BLOSSOM MONTH
For my parents, Sal Cohen and Bep Hartog
Westerbork 20 April 1943 – Sobibor 23 April 1943

April, blossom month
So many years ago

I sit shiva*
in the sun
below the blossom trees
and say kaddish

suddenly the first swallow
flying over
I saw kaddish

flying over
to the past
and my commitment,
my love
carrying with it

to you
in the cattle car
the concentration camp
the gas chamber

April, blossom month
So many years ago

It is over
is it over?

Ellen van der Spiegel Cohen

16

Getting to the bottom of things

So far, I have mainly spoken about the things that have happened to me, based on which I try to trace my live to its earliest beginnings. The causes have now been clearly stated, but do I dare to talk about the consequences for me personally? I decide to do so after long deliberations. Not to create a misplaced sense of compassion but to describe how things work.

The Lower House of Parliament, in the Netherlands, had passed the Prosecution Victims Benefits Act 1940-1945 (WUV) in 1973. People whose physical, mental or psychological health had suffered irreparable damage during the Second World War were eligible for periodic compensation for illnesses or disabilities directly related to the persecution. The application to be 'recognized' as a prosecuted victim had to be substantiated with examination results from medical specialists. I had known for a long time that 'something was wrong with me', that the psychological and emotional problems that manifested themselves had always been latent. The doctors I had visited until then had not been able to come to the right diagnosis.

When Ivonne and I decided, in 1981, to go on aliyah after our lives calmed down because of the sale of my business assets, I found the courage and strength to submit the application for recognition to the PUR (Pension and Benefits Council). In May that year, a social worker of the JMW* came by in Stiens, in the Netherlands, to fill in the necessary forms. She writes the following in her report: 'He clearly has difficulties talking about his psychological problems, he does not want to be ill. He seemed anxious to say something about this.' I only learned this in 2000, when a social worker, Mrs. Paulinka Kreisberg, of the PUR visited me in Israel and came to the same conclusion. She let me read this report from 1981.

We went on aliyah on September 7, 1981, I informed the PUR. Early 1983, I received a message in Israel to make an appointment with psychiatrist dr. Chaim Dasberg in Jerusalem. He had to draw up a psychological report about me for the PUR. A phrase from his report: 'Mr. Louis Godschalk has been ill for some years. He still is and has always been...'

A relative of him, rabbi Nathan Dasberg, who helped me for years in Israel to find my way back to Judaism, insisted, already in the eighties, that I apply for psychotherapeutic help. I did not dare to do that at that time, only because of the stressful concept of 'psychiatric help'. What would anyone else think about me?

The 'recognition' followed on November 3, 1983, provisionally for a period of five years with retroactive effect from 1981. I assumed that this meant that the benefits would also start so that I could close the file. Nothing could be further from the truth, the PUR continued to ask questions, new questions all the time, and ultimately fill eight thick folders. It is December 1985 when the PUR asked me to contact their office in Jerusalem. This same office wrote the following in March of that year: 'You must be patient.' I was waiting for more than four years now and was not allowed to ask when the payment of benefits would start.

The PUR offices in Jerusalem write the following on February 3, 1986: 'You may no longer postpone your visit to our offices.' I postponed this visit for the following reasons:
- I had great difficulty answering questions about my past during previous visits. They were sometimes so intrusive that it made me unwell;
- all previous letters, phone calls and visits were unsuccessful;
- the way the Jerusalem office reported to the offices in the Netherlands took place was at least incomplete.

Even though I was not emotionally ready for it, I visited the PUR offices in Jerusalem. It turned out that I needed to sign the application for WUV benefits after 1986. An additional psychological examination was needed for these follow-up benefits. I did not receive an invitation for this. I did not have the courage or energy to pursue this. The talk with dr. Chaim Dasberg remained stuck in my head for a long time and I had often difficulties sleeping because of it. The talks at the PUR offices in Jerusalem only reinforced this.

At the end of 1987, I met Mr. Rita Cohen from Amsterdam in Israel. Mr. Rita Cohen, as a lawyer, had a lot of experience with matters related to the WUV laws. She was willing to take over the procedure from me, I signed the authorization with a feeling of relief. Thanks to her efforts, the situation quickly resolved itself, but it still took until the beginning of 1990 before the benefits for 1981-1986 belonging to the recognition started.

In January 2001, I followed the advice of Rabbi Nathan Dasberg to ask for psychotherapeutic help. I did this through the PUR. Not because I was ready for it but because I felt it all had become too much for me. I could not overcome the shock I got in 1956, when I heard that my parents were not my real parents, on my own. My request was granted. In May 2001, I had my first therapeutic conversation with dr. Gerard Kreisberg in Herzliya. We had a connection from the start and I trusted him. I am still grateful to him for what he has meant to me. He taught me to lift my blockades. He could not take away the pain but tried to alleviate it. During the often-emotional conversations, he made me understand that it is sometimes better to accept things, no matter how unacceptable they may be. I could cry the tears that had never been cried with him. Accepting does not mean forgiving the people who had done so much harm to my family. It is not up to me to forgive, this is up to the people who have been murdered.

Dr. Gerard Kreisberg discovered that my foster father had put thoughts in my head. I thought whole my life that I had learning difficulties. He asked me if I could bring my CV with me the next time. When he read it, his conclusion was exactly the opposite. But how did I come to that idea? I pondered a lot before I remembered a thing my foster father used to say. He had regularly told me: 'You cannot learn very well, you should leave school and work as a farmer's worker, as I started when I was a young boy'. Unconsciously, I had been believing that all this time.

These therapeutic talks with dr. Gerard Kreisberg did bring the realization that I needed to take action myself to continue to remain eligible for the WUV benefits. I was 'strong' enough for this again.

At the start of 2003, when we, temporarily, lived in our pied-à-terre in Amsterdam because my foster father was suffering from dementia, as a result of which he could no longer organize normal household business and simple bank payments. I met Mrs. Chaja Joseph at the JMW. During this talk, we happened to touch upon my WUV benefits, which had stopped after 1986. She suggested that I should give her my WUV file, so she could take a look at it. I submitted, to the PUR, the follow-up application on her recommendation in May 2003. Doubts struck me again when I was informed by the PUR five months later that they needed more time. I called Mrs. Mr. Rita Cohen to ask her to mediate again. Sadly, she had discontinued her legal practice. Through the JMW, I met Mrs. Mr. Anneke Bierenbroodspot. She lived near us. Thanks to her experience, she managed to become familiar with the manifest rules and conditions of the WUV. It seemed like all requirements had been made stricter. But she was successful, and I received the message in December 2005 that the benefits would resume as of May 2003. Not as of 1986, for the simple reason that I had failed to take action back then. The PUR did not consider my mental incapacity during that period.

At the advice of dr. Kreisberg, I continued the weekly psychotherapeutic talks with a colleague of his in Amsterdam during the period 2003-2008. Mrs. Mr. Bierenbroodspot requested from this psychologist information for her dossier. It contains the following problem analysis:

- he always feels cramped and 'confused';
- he seems tense to me;
- the almost total inhibition of the aggression effect is striking;
- there was no person to get attached to during the first year of hiding. He was possibly also physically neglected.
- the first year and a half of his life was disastrous;
- he was later lovingly accepted by his (later) foster mother. This meeting was potentially life-saving.

I also participated in assertiveness courses at the JMW and attended the JMW discussion group on 'The Child in Hiding'. Just like at the conferences with the same name, I recognized my problems in others. I tried to overcome my fears and not constantly 'go into hiding' by listening and talking. I managed this to a certain extent but will never get rid of this completely.

After I returned to Israel in 2008, I continue to receive psychotherapeutic treatment to this day.

17

A never-ending movie starts all over again

While I could notice some progress in myself, the situation of my foster parents deteriorated. There was also the sad fact that my foster father began more and more to suffer from dementia. The Rienstra's moved to Talma State, a residential care center, in the village of Heeg, Friesland, in 2001. The youngest sister of my mum, aunt Eke, started living when her husband died. She kept an eye on things and called us when there were financial problems due to administrative errors of my foster father.

Coincidentally, she was married to Gerlof Rienstra. He was not a relative of my foster father. Because she was at that time in the phone book, she was often called when someone needed my foster father. She would give them the caller's number and informed him about the reason of the call, but he would never respond. May be, because the relationship between aunt Eke and her brother-in-law was not good. Actually, it had never been good because aunt Eke knew what was going on at our home.

She and her husband, Gerlof Rienstra, have many times expressed their dissatisfaction with the way my foster father treated his wife. They have also expressed their dissatisfaction about his attitude towards me on several occasions. My foster mother informed Aunt Eke and Uncle Gelf. They have clearly expressed their displeasure many times. Therefore, he became annoyed and angry from the moment he saw her.

Since the health of my mama had also begun deteriorating, from 2000, aunt Eke felt very bad that she could not do more for her sister. When aunt Eke visited her, mama would often be crying because she was unable to get a grip on the situation. This is why aunt Eke asked me for help at the end of 2002 as there was nobody else who she could fall back on when it came to support my foster parents. Ivonne and I decided to go back to Amsterdam for a while. The first thing we did was to check on my foster parents in Heeg. Aunt Eke had not exaggerated, the mood was far from pleasant. When I very carefully explained the purpose of our visit, foster father responded as stung by a wasp. Nothing was wrong with him, he did not need any help whatsoever. Immediately he became angry, beat with his fist on the table. How did I get that idea, the financial administration was perfectly all right! It sounds a bit cynical but for a moment I got the feeling of 'that is the man I know.' It was the same when I was still living at home. It was just like being in the same bad movie again. The only difference was that I was now many years older and no longer needed to heed his quirks. His dementia did not make it any easier but only a little more understandable at best. Unfortunately, the underlying tone was still the same: 'I am the boss, I decide what happens.'

The next visit was no different. Ivonne told me she no longer wanted to come with me to visit my foster parents. She saw the attitude of her father-in-law towards me as emotional blackmail and no longer wanted to witness it.

Our time began to run out as our Israeli three-month travel insurance was about to expire. We did realize that solving this problems would take more time. We applied for health insurance for ourselves at a Dutch insurance company as these kinds of trivial matters are essential. This was only possible for Dutch residents. And that is what we did. The pied-à-terre in Amsterdam would be our home base for the time being. Because it had served as a 'office address and pied-a-terre' until now, some things had to be done before it would become a temporarily cozy home. This task could be entrusted to Ivonne as she had done it before.

Back to Heeg. Koos and I managed to become authorized to pay bills to get the financial disorder under control. I made sure that there were always sufficient funds available at the Rabobank in Heeg. One problem was that my foster father, for more than year, kept withdrawing all the cash and we did not know what he was doing with it. He would have to be placed under guardianship to get a grip on this but that is a major move and the procedure would take some time. I decided to close the Rabobank account in Heeg and open a new bankaccount with the Frieslandbank in Leeuwarden.

It had now become 2007. We realized that we did not want to stay in the Netherlands forever and gave ourselves a period of two years to make the tough decisions. First of all, I begun improving the retail premises in Drachten and Sneek. This had to be completed before we would go back Israel. To keep my finger on the pulse of the renovation activities, I spent three weeks in Friesland from Monday to Friday. I visited my foster parents every day during lunch break. The health of my foster father continued to deteriorate. The general practitioner had prescribed medication to make his aggressive behavior less severe. This was only partially effective. There were two walkers in their apartment, I suggested that I try to rent a larger apartment for them. My foster father: 'No need, things are going fine.'

We were called by the acting physician at six o'clock in the evening on June 18, 2007. He was going to contact the general practitioner because he did not trust the health of Mr. Rienstra. The general practitioner arrived a couple of hours later and concluded that my foster father did not respond to any questions. He called me to discuss what to do. He suggested: let us see what happened this night. My foster mother would take care of him during the night or having my foster father admitted to the hospital. I opted for admission. The general practitioner sent him to the hospital. He passed away there on the next day, early in the morning of June 19, 2007. We were happy to be there to support mama and take care of the necessities arising from his death. And, of course, to comfort her. No matter how difficult the marriage may have been, having to say goodbye to the man you have been married to for 61 years is hard. The farewell service took place in the church of Scharnegoutum, where we said goodbye to him in the adjoining cemetery.

It was sad to conclude that the financial disorder was greater than I had thought. The documents I was now able to take with me to Amsterdam showed that a large part of the proceeds from the sale of their house in Stiens was lost. When I contacted the bank, I was told that he had converted a majority in numbered 'bearer certificates'. He did this for fiscal reasons. The bank statements showed that withdrawals had been made using some of these certificates. However, 80% had never been used and could not be found. Apparently, he had 'cleaned them up' during the periods his dementia was getting worse.

18

Completing the circle

Ivonne and I could now continue with our plans to go back to Israel, this time permanently. For the time being, we planned to depart mid-2008. Of course, we would stay for another year to assist mama with everything.

What to do with the retail premises? The improvements had ensured that we no longer needed to worry about maintenance for the time being. If something was wrong or had to be arranged, Koos would take care of this just like he had done from 1981.

Ivonne had heard from 2002 till 2008, my telephone conversations I had with tenants or other parties. She got a good impression of what was involved. She thought I should no longer burden Koos with this. Koos and I had also passed the age of sixty.

Ivonne thought selling would be the best option. Managing the proceeds from the sale would be enough work for both of us, I did not need to be afraid of 'falling into a void'. The decision was still difficult for me, for the simple reason that the proceeds, which you could consider the award for hard work, specially through the excellent daily care of Koos, were much higher than whatever other investment. Specially we almost knew at the beginning of the year, we were able to calculate what the results would be. The only risk involved was repairs, most of them where insured. After much deliberation and consultation with Koos, we decided to sell the properties. Both the shops and the pied-à-terre.

Once people learned that the properties were for sale, we soon started to receive letters from interested parties. I did not come to an agreement because their offers were always too low. If I had known the financial crisis would erupt in 2009, I might have accepted one of these offers. I indirectly learned the name of a potential buyer who already had several properties in Friesland in his portfolio. I called him on a Wednesday morning October 24, 2008. Around 11 o'clock. I informed him about the bottom price. He was interested, and I immediately sent him extensive information by e-mail. I told him that on Friday, early in the morning, we would leave for visiting our children in Israel for one month. He called back that afternoon around 16.30. Ivonne and I were golfing with her brother Rob. We completed the deal by phone. I provided him with all the files the next morning and we both signed the sale/purchase agreement, he had prepared. This sounds a bit like an adventure. However, this is not a fantasy, only fantastic. As I said, the sale would not have taken place like this after 2008 and we were lucky.

The deed would be executed at the civil-law notary in Amsterdam on 1 April 2008, which meant that we had a couple of months to arrange matters. That was a good thing, as a number of things needed to be settled with the tax authorities because of the death of my foster father. At the tax office, the paper work of the death of my foster father got a couple of time lost, scans were ineligible, and a number of other things went wrong at the tax office. This case only popped up one day before our departure in June 16, 2008.

Ivonne and I had already decided that we wanted to live in the senior complex of the Mediterranean Sea Towers in Nordiya in due course. We had been there often, good friends of us starts to live there in 2001. The houses were to the small side. I did not want to have my desk in the living room again – like in Amsterdam. In 2007, we visited friends who also lived there. 'Coincidentally', someone from the 'Sales' department came by. She had heard that we were interested and informed us that larger houses would be built, which would be completed in a year. In June 2008, we rented a house in Tel Mond, near Nordiya, for one year.

The construction went as we were told, and we could move in a year later. Four rooms and an attic, the attic I have furnished as an office. The complex is walled in and is close to some larger places, which means that all everyday amenities are at hand. There are plenty of recreational and cultural facilities. I am often in the gym or do a few laps in the pool., sauna and jacuzzi.

The staff includes doctors and nurses. Nowadays, you would call something like this 'life-cycle proof'. We had to get used to life in Israel, especially when it came to the language. 'How do you say this again, what do they mean by this?' It was difficult, we may have been in the Netherlands for too long.

I called mama every day, sometimes twice per day, and she was happy to talk with me each time. I did notice after a while that she could remember less and less and that she was slower to respond to a question. The specter of dementia also appeared in her. She was occasionally admitted to the hospital in Sneek when her health deteriorated. Geertje Dijkstra and Koos then went to visit her and kept me informed. The general practitioner thought it was sufficient that the district nurses regularly went to see her. Unfortunately, that was not enough, and she would fall and suffer from fractures. When she was taking to the hospital her dementia would exacerbate due to the anesthesia.

She could no longer go back to Talma State. Mama had to be admitted to the residential, care and treatment center the Ielânen, also in Sneek. The care there was more than excellent. Lots of good is possible if the well-being of the patient is paramount. They also value contact with family and friends. When aunt Eke wanted to go to her sister, her son Gerlof would bring her. Geertje and Geert Dijkstra from Stiens would also mean a lot to mama during that period. When I was getting married, Geertje had lived with my foster parents for a year to study an additional year at the Protestant Teacher College in Leeuwarden.

Geertje and Geert later moved to Stiens, where she met the Rienstra's again. They have always kept in touch after that. When a health progress meeting was held at the Ielânen, Geertje would attend it on my behalf, after which she would inform Koos and me of the unfortunate decline of mama. I could ask a nurse questions when I was on the phone with mama. These were not positive messages. Mama did remain interested in Ivonne and the grandchildren and great-grandchildren up to the end.

The life of my special and dear mama came to an end on December 14, 2011. I became an orphan for the second time when I was sixty-nine years old. We flew back to the Netherlands at the first opportunity. There was no time to send out written invitations, we had to suffice with an advertisement in the Friesch Dagblad and an e-mail to family and friends who we wanted to inform. The funeral ceremony was held in Scharnegoutum on December 21, 2011, the town where she was born on April 2, 1919.

It was wonderful to see how many people had come to pay the last tribute and respect to mama. Among them my school friends from Scharnegoutum. I had kept in touch with them and they also attended the funeral of my foster father. It was nice that they made the effort again.

Mrs. Ellen Kuiper-Groeneveld – pastor at Talma State – led the service for Henderika Rienstra-Oosterkamp in the Martenstsjerke in Scharnegoutum, in a beautiful and respectful way. Lighting a candle 'for the love given by the deceased during her life which will not be lost' was impressive. The focus is now on the deceased, not the strict rules of the church.

The light wooden coffin with mama's picture on top of it stands in the center aisle, next to a bouquet of flowers. The coffin was surrounded with tables with the certificate of Yad Vashem, the Yad Vashem medal, the certificate of her Honorary Citizenship of the State of Israel, and copies of articles in newspapers about her Yad Vashem ceremony.

Besides the usual parts of the service – signing, prayers, and reading from the Bible (Psalm 84:1-5 and John 14:1-3), the creed, and the thoughts of the pastor, there was also room for some personal words from me. I had a pleasant exchange of views on this with Mrs. Kuiper-Groeneveld.

The organist first played the national anthem of Israel, Hatikva – the Hope.

I was then given the floor. I first thanked everyone who had been near to mama, especially in the last period of her life. I then talked about how I was cared for in the Oosterkamp family as a baby and the significant risks that entailed. Just think of the time when 'Gerrit' was brought to safety by crossing the Zwette in a rowing boat, just like Moses in the wicker basket on the Nile.

I also referred to the protection, love and care she had given me. Her personality: helpful, cheerful, lovable, commitment to our private and business activities, the activities in our family.

'Mama, losing you hurts. We are grateful that you could stay with us for so long. May the memory of you, as 'Righteous among the Nations' be a blessing to all of us.'

We then we put her to rest in her grave, next to that of her husband. This completed the circle for both of them.

19

Stolpersteine

'Stolpersteine' is a project by visual artist Gunter Demnig. He was born in Berlin in 1947 and grew up there. His father had been a member of the NSDAP* during the war. Gunter was not involved in this and did not share the views of this organization at all. In hindsight, he was part of the protest generation of the sixties as a visual artist: anti-militarist, pacifist, and politically left-wing. His artistic work is aimed at connecting people, denouncing injustice, and striving for peace.

Demnig brings memorials on the pavement in front of the former houses of people who have been expelled, deported, murdered or committed suicide by the Nazis. These Stolpersteine are reminders of Jews, Sinti and Roma, political prisoners, conscientious objectors, homosexuals, Jehovah's witnesses and the disabled. The artist calls them Stolpersteine because you stumble over it with your head and your heart, and you have to bow to read the text.

On the stones, in a brass plate, the name, date of birth, date of deportation, place and date of death are stamped. The small stones (10 x 10 cm) were all made and placed by the artist himself for a long time. Due to the stormy development of the project, he is now supported by the friendly sculptor Michael Friedrich-Friedländer.

He placed a stone with a brass plate in front of the town hall of his home town Cologne on December 16, 1992. On that day, it was fifty years ago Himmler ordered the deportation of thousand Roma and Sinti. The plate displays the first lines of this order (Auschwitz Decree). On January 4, 1995, he placed the first stolperseine in Cologne without permission of the authorities. The brass plate (10 x 10 cm) shows the name, date of birth, date of deportation, place and date on which they died. The official start of the Stolpersteine Project took place in 2000.

The initiative was a huge success. Demnig initially aimed to place a few hundred stones, he and his employees had already placed about 69,000 stones in more than 21 countries by mid-2018. Most of the Stolpersteine are placed for murdered Jews. Demnig also expressly envisaged that, as far he is concerned, the stones are for *all* the victims of Nazi terror.

The first stones in the Netherlands were placed in Borne on November 29, 2007.

Demnig strives to personally place the stones as much as possible. The 'Spuren-Gunther Demnig' foundation was established in 2015 to ensure that 'the work' can continue even if Demnig can no longer do it himself. Demnig has received several awards for his work.

2014. Stolpersteine

The idea really appealed to us. I contacted Mr. De Haan, coordinator for Amsterdam, and submitted my request for two stones in front of the house where my parents and I lived. He contacted Gunther Demnig who approved my request. On April 15, 2014 – 70 years and a day after

I was brought to the Oosterkamp family – Ivonne and I were standing in front of the house at Réaumurstraat 22 together with family, friends and acquaintances. The current residents and their neighbors joined the group. Seeing Demnig kneels to place two stones in the pavement with the names, dates of birth, date of deportation, and the date on which my parents were murdered is an emotional moment for me. My parents had spent their short marriage in relative freedom here. I was born here and together we were betrayed and taken to the Hollandsche Schouwburg, where they made the impossible heroic decision to say goodbye to me to give me a chance of life.

Here am I, dear mother and dad!
Thank you for choosing to give me life.
Thank you for your love and care.
Ivonne and I were granted a daughter and a son,
we named them after you.

Bind their souls in the bundle of eternal life.
Let their souls rest in peace where their remains are.
They have not been forgotten.
They will never be forgotten.

Also see: https://www.youtube.com/watch?v=eGgb-4euRJs

20

Questions and answers

Is there a clear answer to the question 'Who am I?'

I must conclude that this is *not* the case. The stones have been placed at the house where I may *not* have been born. This doubt comes from reading my OPK file. I have left this as it was for a long time but could not let it go. Because DNA testing became increasingly prominent during the years, I hoped that a test would provide a definite answer. Finally, I contacted dr. Ron Loewenthal MD PhD, an expert in this field. He is connected to the Sheba Medical Center in Tel Aviv. I submitted my 'question' to him.

His answer can be summarized as follows: Mitochondrial DNA passed from the mother to her female and male offspring. Assuming Anna Zwaaf is my real mother, I am her only surviving descendant. My sister Cornelia died at a very young age. My mother had one sister, Lena. She was also murdered in the war and had no descendants. My grandmother, Clara Zwaaf, had one sister, Anna, who also did not have any offspring. I cannot pursue this line of testing.

When testing the male line, researchers look at the Y chromosome. This passes from father to son. Despite all my research, I cannot make any headway here. Only two second or grandnieces in Australia are still alive of my Godschalk family. They should have been second nephews for this test to work.

The editors of the Spoorloos program did not succeed in finding family members of the 'Godschalk branch' in 1994.

In the years that I have left, I will no longer occupy myself with the question 'who am I?'.

I have always proudly borne the name Godschalk and will continue to do so.

21

We count our blessings

The unique bond between Jews and the land of Israel is constantly repeated in our prayers, blessings, and feasts. Israel is the air we breathe. Jews always have a constant and strong desire for it for our almost 2000 years of exile. The Scriptures, especially in Leviticus and Jeremiah, are filled with promises, hope and comfort, true music for the future. 'The children will return to their own borders, they will return from the land of the enemy. There will be sounds of joy and happiness.' And: 'As the Lord says: Keep your voice from weeping, and your eyes from tears, for there is a reward for your work. Yes, there is hope for your future, the children will return to their land.'

Throughout Jewish history, the open question has been whether Jews suffered the most losses from: the bitter poison of anti-Semitism* or the sweet poison of assimilation. Victims of both disappear from the scene of Jewish history. In my case, both anti-Semitism and assimilation were closely linked. What was done to my family could not be undone but my assimilation could be corrected because we have our own state, Israel. For the first time in 2000 years, we Jews have the privilege of choosing to go on aliyah to our own country, Eretz Israel! Back to our roots. Striving to replant in our children what was almost cut off by the Nazis.

I felt strongly and deeply that I was Jewish, without any Jewish education. My identity did not come from Auschwitz but from the Sinai, from the covenant between the Lord and Moses and His mission for Him and the people. Our children and grandchildren will not have to feel Jewish because of what happened to their families during the Shoah. They will only feel Jewish if they are motivated and inspired to remain Jewish. From generation to generation. The massacre of my family by the Nazis is not the only reason for our aliyah. Above all, Ivonne and I wished to ensure our children a Jewish future. This is why Ivonne and I tried to connect Amelek with Jethro, devastation to revelation, destruction to revelation, an almost lost Jewish generation to the new generation. A Jewish upbringing for our children: we believed that the only guarantee to realize the progress of my Judaism is to pass on the Jewish tradition to our children. From generation to generation.

Zalman Shazar, the third president of Israel, a historian, said:

'A generation cannot possibly pass anything on to the next
if they have not received it correctly from the previous generation'.

And:

Abraham Burg, Member of the Israeli Parliament for many years, said:

'Let us, Jews, live, work and Pray as Israelis in Israel, which means:
We will not forget the past,
but we live in the present,
and trust in the future.'

Our children have developed into fully-fledged members of Israeli society. Both have completed their military service in the Israeli army, Anna Vanessa for two years and Lion Patrick his three. We are proud of this. Anna Vanessa and Lion Patrick decided in 1992 to 'come out' (to become Jewish) according to the Israeli Orthodox requirements. Rabbi Avishay Daum, Director of the Institute for 'Judaic Studies' in Ramat Gan, advised and indicated how they would be able to realize their giyur*.

'Coming out' (doing giyur)*, means that, according to the Israeli Orthodox requirements, that if Anna Vanessa and Lion Patrick marry, they would be able to receive a Jewish Orthodox chuppah, which means that their children will be recognized as Jews. Lion Patrick must marry a Jewish woman because Judaism is based on the identity of the mother. The fact that Anna Vanessa and Lion Patrick did this of their own free will was an extremely important victory over the Nazis for me. They had failed to destroy my Jewish generation. Ivonne and I had brought two Jews, two future worlds, back into the covenant of Abraham, Isaac and Jacob.

'And Moses stretched out his hand over the sea, and all that night G'd drove the sea back with a strong east wind and turned it into dry land and the waters were divided.'

The Babylonian Talmud states that bringing people together in marriage is harder than dividing the Red Sea. According to our Jewish sages, marriage is a miracle. Marriage gives hope, strangers become one. Each marriage ceremony ends with the prayer for salvation.

On 20 January 1998, we celebrated the chuppah (Jewish Religious Blessing of the marriage) of Lion Patrick with Sigal Nachum, a Jewish woman of Iraq-Kurdish descent. We were delighted with the addition of this family-in-law. On October 13, 1998, we celebrated the chuppah of Anna Vanessa and Eli Elazer, a Jewish man whose parents come from Iraq. The family circle has become more international.

Each marriage ceremony rightly ends with the prayer for salvation: that, as Jeremiah says, the sounds of joy and happiness, the sounds of the bride and groom, may soon be heard in the cities of Judea and on the squares of Jerusalem. As far we were concerned, the wish of Jeremiah was heard. The children have returned. It did not stop there: five grandchildren were born, and we celebrated three Bar Mitzvahs* and two Bat Mitzvahs*. I personally also wish to do Bar Mitzvah one day.

We celebrated 'brit milah, ritual circumcision, three times. I once was the sandek, the person who is honored at the ceremony, at the brit milah of Ron. The sandek has the baby on his laps when the brit milah is being carried out. The break in my Jewish family tradition has now been repaired. I can now go to the synagogue with my son, daughter and grandsons, something my father and grandfathers have never been able to do. All the more reason for Ivonne and me to feel as proud and grateful Jewish parents and grandparents of our five grandchildren.

Children are the future for Israel. The economic, diplomatic and military strength rests on two pillars that are an extension of each other.

First and most important: the children in Israel and their education. The need to ensure that the education of our children transfers into a living Jewish identity. The second pillar is linked to this: The Israel Defense Force (IDF), the Israeli army. Boys enter the army at the age of eighteen for three years and refresh their training annually. This period is two years for girls, they do not need to annually refresh their training after this period. These boys and girls make the IDF one of the most powerful armies in the world.

I count my blessings:
- Born in a Jewish family;
- My parents let me go into hiding, this heroic deed saved my life;
- Mama, my new mother; who also saved my life;
- Rabbi Slagter sends me to the almud Torah school in Amsterdam; where Rabbi Jitschak Mundstück introduced me into Judaism;
- Max Abram, a friend, like a father, my mentor, an example, unconditionally prepared to grant selfless help;
- Ivonne, who agreed to marrying her;
- Anna Vanessa and Lion Patrick, our children;
- Shiraz, Ron, Ady, Iron and Idor, our grandchildren;
- Koos Boorsma: I cannot put into words what he means for Ivonne and me since 1981;
- Aliyah in 1981;
- Enjoying life every day, together with Ivonne.

Words of gratitude and appreciation

In the introduction to this autobiography, I wrote:

'I dedicate this book to you, my murdered Jewish parents and you, my murdered Jewish family.'

There are people whom I want to honor, thank, and who I can never show enough respect for their love, friendship, attention, and selfless help.

- First, my parents, from November 1, 1942 until mid-July 1943, Z"L" *
- My foster mother, my mama, Hennie Oosterkamp, from April 14, 1944 until December 14, 2011†.
- Bea and Wim Polak* from the early fifties. Bea until 2006, Z"L"; Wim until 1987, Z"L".
- Ivonne Geertruida de Graeve, from February 23, 1964.
- The parents of Ivonne from February 24, 1964. Cornelia until 1987†, Jacob until 1977†.

I want to express thanks to:
- Mr. Drs. Herman Vandormael and Mr. Hajo Smit. Without their comments, remarks, and substantive recommendations, Koos and I would not have been able to realize this autobiography.
- Thanks to the team Uitgeverij Aspekt, particularly Mr. W. Pierik sr. and Mr. P. Pierik, who expressed their enthusiasm and craftsmanship in usual recommendations.
- Thanks to Mr. B.J. Film for checking some historical data.
- Last but no least: thanks to Mike Rodrigue for his 'translate assistance'.

I would like to take this opportunity to thank five persons who have a special place in my life:
- Max Abram. Max was brought during the war to the Abma family as an evacuee. He visited me at the Oosterkamp family during bread deliveries in 1944/1945. I had the honor to work in his clothing company after my military service. He assisted me and Ivonne to start my own Mantelhuis in 1965 without any conditions. I was able to set up a successful chain of seven fashion stores in the period 1965 to 1979 with his help and advice.
- Koos Boorsma, from 1981, my agent, and advisor, as well as in 2018, the editor of my biography. I want to thank Koos for his endless patience, his energy, his ongoing expert advice, from 1981 to today. He has 'translated' the numerous hours of reading my biography writings, (telephone) conversations about the history of my life over a period of many months into a readable story.
- Anna Vanessa and Lion Patrick, for the joy that Ivonne and I experience by being your parents.
- Shiraz, Ady, Ron, Idor and Iron, of which Ivonne and I are the proud grandparents.
- Finally, last but not at least, I want to thank Ivonne, my special love since 1964.

Without her understanding, compassion, patience, love, zeal, and attention.

Dear Ivonne, we have spent more time together than many other couples have had. However, time is relative. It is about what we experience and do during this time, each for himself or herself.

In South Africa, they say:
'We do not dream, we live this dream'

I cannot describe my gratitude to you.
The beautiful life you have given me cannot be described.
Spending more than 54 years together involves a type
of art of survival.

We never had one dull moment.
We together fought for a solid future for us and for our children with the greatest possible integrity.

This is and remains unforgettable for me.

Mediterranean Sea Towers Nordiya
Israel 2018

Appendix 1

A vision

I wrote the following a few years ago:

Every history has an end.
Life is also finite.
And becoming older is part of life.

Occasionally, when I see my grandchildren play,
I get the thought: they should not have been here…

I think that they and I are only alive thanks to a combination of luck and privilege.

All in all, life has spoiled me!
I thank G'd for every day He has given me.
Even though I always feel a sadness that never runs out.
I want to thank Ivonne from the bottom of my heart for the wonderful life I still have with her.
We have already celebrated our golden anniversary.

Sometimes,
An angel appears to me,
the angel shows my parents and grandparents the daily life
of Ivonne and me and of our beloved children and grandchildren.
How we speak Ivrit with each other, how we watch Israeli television,
Criticize our Prime Minister, attend the synagogue.

Then I hear my parents and grandparents ask:
'Is this reality or is it a dream?'
The angel answers:
'This is real.'
The eyes of my parents and all four of my grandparents – bless their memory – grow wide.

They say as if with one mouth: 'Then the Messiah has come to Earth!'

Appendix 2

From generation to generation – Le Dor Va Dor

Shortly before he dies, Ya'acov blesses the two sons of Joseph, his grandchildren.
In other words, a father in the Jewish tradition is not only responsible for
the future of his children but indirectly also for his grandchildren.
This is also an important reason for our Aliyah.

The time Ya'acov would die was approaching.
He summoned his son Joseph.
Joseph understood the state of health of his father.
Joseph brought his two sons to the bed his father was lying on.
Ya'avoc told Joseph that his two sons,
both born in Egypt, are as dear to him as his own sons.

Then Ya'acov blesses Joseph his sons, Ephraim and Menasheh:

For boys, the introductory line is:
May you be like Ephraim and Menasheh.
Jesiemega Ello-hiem ke'Ephraim wegimena'sjè.

For girls, the introductory line is:
May you be like Sarah, Rebecca, Rachel, and Leah.
Jesiemeeg Ello-hiem kesara rivka racheel welee'h

For both boys and girls, the rest of the blessing is:
May God bless you and guard you.
May God show you favor and be gracious to you.
May God show you kindness and grant you peace.
jesiemega Ello-hiem ke'Ephraim wegimena'sjè.

Why Ehphraim and Menasheh
They are the sons of Joseph and Osnat.
Ya'acov blessed them, also on behalf of his father Yitzschak and
his grandfather Abraham, before he died.
His son Joseph was viceroy in morally poor Egypt.
Ephraim and Menasheh were born in Egypt.

Despite this handicap, Joseph succeeded in preserving the monotheistic vision and the associated way of life of his ancestors.

Ya'acov blessing was that they should be a blessing, an example to the Jewish people for all time. From that day forward, they would become role models for Jewish children everywhere, as they represented qualities to emulate eternally.
Ephraim and Menasheh were the first brothers among our forefathers to live without rivalry. Before them came Isaac and Ishmael, *Ya'acov* and Esau, and, of course, Joseph's brothers who sold him as a slave, all relationships fraught with conflict and competition.
Ephraim and Menasheh were brothers who lived in harmony, for their life focus was the highest example of working for good for their community and people.
Their decisions were not based on, *what is good for me?* but on, *what is good for the Jewish people?*
Concerns of ego were cast aside in favor of something greater.
The words of King David ring true: 'How good and pleasant is it for brothers to sit peacefully together.'

(Psalms 133:1). This is the hope that God holds for all the Jewish people.

Ivonne her father was called Ya'acov,
Ivonne chose the Jewish name Osnat for herself.

An important lesson in Jewish history is
that we look at the future from the present.
Present and past are both present in the future.

From generation to generation – **Le Dor Va Dor**

Appendix 3

In memoriam Hendrika Rienstra-Oosterkamp
Scharnegoutum 2 April 1919 – Heeg 14 December 2011 †

Praising her life, in the church of her youth in Scharnegoutum, we read Psalm 84. This psalm talks about how good it is to be in the house of the Lord and how the soul yearns to be there. We read in John 14 how Jesus promised His disciples to prepare a house in 'the House of my Father'.

Hennie Rienstra was a woman who lived to help others. She was the oldest at home and when her mother died at a young age, she naturally took over the care of her two younger brothers and sister. It was 14 April 1944 when a gentleman with a one-and-a-half-year-old boy knocked at their door. It turned out to be a Jewish child who needed shelter. And just like the 'swallow and the sparrow' find a home in Psalm 84, this boy, called Louis Godschalk, found a safe space in the Oosterkamp home.

When her father remarried, she had found a partner and married Feike Rienstra in November 1945. Louis went with them and when it became clear that his parents had not survived the war, he was adopted. By taking in a Jewish child during the war, she, and posthumously her father, received a Yad Vashem award in 1981. She was invited to plant a tree at the Avenue of the Righteous on the Mount of Remembrance in Jerusalem with a sign with her name and the name of her father. A tribute by the State of Israel to people who saved someone of Jewish descent during the Second World War.

Eight years later, in April 1989, she received another invitation from Yad Vashem to come to Jerusalem. This time she would be granted honorary citizenship of the State of Israel. The simple and modest Hendrika Rienstra-Oosterkamp was the fourth person in the world to be included in the erudite company of the greatest persons of Earth. She was a 'Righteous among the Nations' because she had put her life at risk by taking in a defenseless Jewish boy in her home. Her name is on a plaque in Israel so that we will not forget the righteous of the world.

In the tribute service for her life, Louis said the kaddish prayer for her, the Hebrew prayer for a deceased parent. He had been unable to do so for his own parents but could now express his love and gratitude for her in this special manner. A moving experience.

I hope that Hennie Rienstra-Oosterkamp, 'Righteous among the Nations', has found a place to live forever where she may sing her songs of praise for the God she loved so much.

Her name will not be forgotten, as it is engraved in the palm of the hand of God.

Ellen Kuiper-Groeneveld, pastor

Appendix 4

In memoriam for my 'mama'

Pastor Mrs. Ellen Kuiper-Groeneveld. Ladies of the Plantein and the Ielânen Residential, Care and Treatment Center. Ladies of Home Care. Ladies of Talma State. Aunt Eke, Baukje and Gerlof. The Stellingwerf-Elzinga family. Elly Hessel, Sjoukje, Koos, Eric en Eddy Boorsma, Geertje and Geert Dijkstra, Eelke Boersma and Archan Zijlstra, Anne van der Laan-Droogsma, Ger and Gosse Bootsma, Dieuwke Hendriksma, Klaasje Rienstra, Sjoerd and Jelly Zondervan-Rienstra, Sipke and Maaike van der Velde-Rienstra, Alko and Tineke Vlap-Bootsma,

Dear family, my school friends from the Dutch Reformed elementary school in Scharnegoutum, Ate Jellema, Freek Haan and Joost Schaap, present here. Ladies and gentlemen: thank you for coming, for making the effort to accompany mama to her final resting place. Thank you, also on behalf of mama.

Farewell

During the fearful, frightened and dark years of the Second World War, I was an eighteen months old Jewish baby when I was taken into the family of Klaas Oosterkamp and his children; Hennie, Marten, Siebe and Eke. This was a life-threatening act of resistance by Klaas Oosterkamp and his children at that time. Klaas Oosterkamp, his wife, Ruurdje Boersma, had died two years before and Hennie, his oldest daughter, now took care of the household. This was a beautiful and loving time for me, as Hennie cared for me with her sister Eke and her brothers Marten and Siebe.

This is how I gained my second mother on April 14, 1944 as a Jewish child in hiding. I was not the first Jewish child to be 'hidden' for an enemy intent on killing Jewish children. The first child was Moses, the son of Jochebed and the Levite* Amram, who was hidden in a wicker basket from the Pharaoh of Egypt, who had all newborn Jewish children murdered during that time.

The feeling of justice Klaas Oosterkamp and his children gave me during the Second World War was continued by mama (Hennie) after the war. My family did not come to pick me up immediately after the war.

Hennie married Feike Rienstra on November 8, 1945. Hennie and Feike temporarily took me into their new family. In the course of time, it became clear that my own Jewish parents and all close relatives had been murdered in a brutal, inhumane and beastly manner by the supporters of National Socialism and mama and Feike adopted me and accepted me into their family.

Mama, Ivonne and our children Anna Vanessa and Lion Patrick and I never appealed to you in vain, the interests of your neighbor, the 'other', was your first priority. You were helpful, mama, you were cheerful, you were a sweet and lovable person, you loved the highlights in your and our lives.

Like in 1981, during your ceremony at Yad Vashem in Jerusalem where you and your father Klaas Oosterkamp posthumously, on behalf of the whole Oosterkamp family, were offered the Yad Vashem award from the State of Israel.

Like in 1986, in Jerusalem again, at your ceremony where you, as the fourth person in the world, were appointed Honorary Citizen of the State of Israel.

The 'Monument for the Hidden Child and Protector' in Amsterdam-Buitenveldert is a bronze statue of a male figure who embraces a girl. He holds her suitcase in his hand. The sculpture is placed on a natural stone pedestal, on which a memorial plaque is placed. The whole is on a square. The memorial is 1 meter 30 high, 5 meters 20 wide and 8 meters 50 deep.

When Ivonne and I were in the Netherlands, we lived in our pied-à-terre in Amsterdam-Buitenveldert. The statue of 'the Jewish child in hiding and his protector' can be found in Buitenveldert. This statue was founded by the Dutch 'Jewish Child in Hiding' foundation. It will always remind people of the courage and sacrifice of people like your father Klaas Oosterkamp, yourself, aunt Eke, uncle Marten, and uncle Siebe.

Mama, you were present at all our festive private and business activities. Mama, because you have reached the age of the strong, you have seen your two grandchildren, Anna Vanessa and Lion Patrick; get married.

Mama, you were always interested in your five great-grandchildren and asked about them. Mama, losing you hurts. May the memory of you be a blessing. In my Jewish tradition, the children of the deceased say a kaddish prayer. I was not able to say a kaddish prayer for my own biological parents when they were murdered in Sobibor on July 23, 1943.

Now that you, my second mama, passed away, I take the liberty as a Jewish (foster) child to say this kaddish prayer now that I have become an orphan for the second time. The kaddish prayer in which G'd's Greatness and Might is expressed. The Jewish kaddish prayer is a hymn to G'd's kingship. This kaddish prayer does not contain any words about death, no references to dying, no phrases about suffering, it is a hymn to G'd in which all grief melts away.

The opening text in English is as follows: 'Glorified and sanctified be His great Name throughout the world which He has created according to His will and may He establish His kingdom in your lifetime and during your days, and within the life of the entire House of Israel, speedily and soon. And say: Amen*. May His great Name be blessed forever and to all eternity.' The text concludes with 'He who creates peace in His celestial heights, may He create peace for us and for all Israel. And say: Amen.' In Ivrit: 'Jitgadal wejitkadasj, sjemee rabba. Be'olma die wera chiroetei wejamliech malchoete, bechajjechon oewejomegon decol bet jisraël, ba'agalla oewizman kariew, we iemroe: amen. Ose shalom bimromov hoe ja'asee shalom alenoe we'al kol Jisraël we iemroe: amen.'

And to end my speech, Channa Szenes*, an Israeli poetess, wrote: 'There are stars whose light reaches the Earth only long after they themselves have disintegrated.

There are people whose memory gives light in this world long after they have passed away from us. This light shines in the darkest night on the path we have to take.'

Shalom, dear mama, leg ba shalom/rest in peace. Amen.

Louis Godschalk

Appendix 5

The kaddish prayer

The kaddish prayer is the confession and unconditional acceptance of G'd's leadership over the world, both for the whole and for the individual. This in all circumstances of life, even if we have to sacrifice our lives to acknowledge it. This is why this confession is also said when we face the great mystery of death, when we need to ask ourselves 'why'. The heart of the prayer is to speak it publicly, with 'minjan' (the ten Jewish men required to jointly perform the prayer) and glorifying what G'd means to us. A meaning that is laid down in the four-letter Name, which mean can be said to be: *Who there was, Who there is, Who there always will be.*

Originally, this prayer was spoken after a speech in which the traditions are handed down to the congregation using Biblical sites and to which a word of comfort with the Messianic idea was associated. It originated during the Babylonian exile. The vernacular at that time was Aramaic. Even though there are sources that give a somewhat similar text in Hebrew, the text of our kaddish prayer is in Aramaic.

The prayer has five different forms.
- Kaddish Shalom: the entire kaddish, spoken by the reader after the end of a main prayer.
- Hatzi-Kaddish: half kaddish, only the first two strophes, spoken by the reader after the end of a certain part of the service.
- Kaddish-Yatom: (orphan's prayer) spoken by someone who is in the year of mourning for his parents or on the 'annual day'.
- Kaddish-Derabenan: with a special prayer for rabbinic scholars, spoken after learning.

- Kaddish-le(it)chadda: spoken at a funeral and ends of sections of the Talmud* with another text of the first part, starting with the word: le(it)chaddata.

Cantor:
Glorified and sanctified be His great Name throughout the world which He has created, according to His will and may He establish His kingdom in your lifetime and during your days, and within the life of the entire House Israel, speedily and soon. And say: Amen*.

Congregation:
May His great Name be blessed forever and to all eternity.

Cantor:
Blessed and praised, glorified and exalted, extolled and honored, adored and lauded be the name of the Holy One, blessed be He, beyond all the blessings and hymns, praises and consolations that are ever spoken in the world; And say: Amen.

Congregation:
Accept our prayer mercifully and benevolently!

Cantor:
May there be abundant peace from heaven, and life, for us and for all Israel; And say: Amen.

Congregation:
The Name of the Eternal One is praised from now and to all eternity.

Cantor:
He who creates peace in His celestial heights, may He create peace for us and for all Israel; And say: Amen.

Congregation:
My help comes from the Eternal One, the creator of heaven and earth.

Appendix 6

Yad Vashem award for Hendrika Rienstra-Oosterkamp and Klaas Oosterkamp 30 March 1981

Ladies and gentlemen.
Today my mama, Mrs. Hendrika (Hennie) Rienstra-Oosterkamp, will receive the Yad Vashem award, also for her deceased father, Klaas. Mama will plant a tree, also on behalf of her father, at the Avenue of the Righteous on the Mount of Remembrance in Jerusalem. Because Klaas and Hennie Oosterkamp hid me during the war, risking their own lives, so that the Germans did not kill me like almost all my other family members.

I wish you all a warm welcome to this Yad Vashem ceremony. What can, and should I say today? It should not be too long, brief with content, while it may not distract from what is actually at stake this morning. For those of you who do not know the history of the Oosterkamp family, Rienstra and me, I will give a brief summary, followed by something about the war, which has brought us all here.

I was born in Amsterdam on November 1, 1942. My parents had gone into hiding shortly after I was born. We were betrayed, arrested, and taken to the collection point in Amsterdam at the Plantage Middenlaan, the Hollandsche Schouwburg. We had to wait for transport to transit camp Westerbork in the Hollandsche Schouwburg. The actions of my parents at the beginning of the war tell me that my parents, like so many others, had no idea what Nazi anti-Semitism* was capable of.

But who can understand it, condemning people to death only for being Jewish? Ninety-nine percent of the Jews never chose to be Jews, they were born in this way. You cannot change this, even if you wanted to. I asked my teacher, Rabbi Jitschak Mundstück at the Talmud Torah school in Amsterdam, about this, and he answered: 'You are born without your permission and you die without your permission.'

Mrs. Hester van Lennep smuggled me out of the Jewish daycare opposite the Hollandsche Schouwburg in July 1943. My war file only tells me that I was brought to the Van der Goot family at Gootzand 57 in Sneek. I was later brought to the Klaas Dijkstra family in the Sacramentsstraat in Sneek. My last hiding address was with the Klaas Oosterkamp family in Scharnegoutum. A small village, three kilometer outside Sneek. After the death of Mrs. Ruurdje Oosterkamp, the mother of Hennie, Hennie gave up her job at the end of 1941 to take over the household of her father. The family consisted of Hennie, as the oldest daughter, Marten, Siebe, and Eelkje. Hennie became my new mother, in other words, I did not know any better than that Hennie was my mother.

Hendrika Oosterkamp and Feike Rienstra: the war was over and a lot of young, as well as old, couples married in the fall of 1945. I imagine how Feike suggested Hennie that they marry. Hennie would have said: 'Yes, I will, but you will get 'Gerrit' (as I was called back then) as well'. Hennie had grown attached to me. Her father also married again in the fall of 1945. Hennie did not want to expose me to another 'mother' again.

I grew up in Scharnegoutum believing that I was a child of Feike and Hennie. I knew the word 'mama' already when I was brought to Hennie in April 1944. Mama, and later Feike, submitted a request for adoption to continue to take care of me. The court appointed the Rientras as guardians. As a child, just like any other child, I had a father, a mother and grandparents, uncles, aunts, nephews and nieces on both sides.

Things did not change, when I married Ivonne. Ivonne and I opened our first ladies fashion store in Sneek in 1965. Mama helped in our store. More stores followed, as well as two children. Mama would look after the children and my foster father became our accountant. Mama started peeling one extra potato for a baby and would do 50 years later the same for four, these are the beautiful things in life.

I think of Genesis, of the second dream of Joseph, in which he tells his father and his brothers that the son, the moon and the elf stars bow down before him. Father Jacob reprimands him and says: 'What a dream. Should we, I, your mother, and your brothers come to bow for you as well?' Joseph his brothers envied him, and his father Jacob kept the matter in mind. Jacob wanted to divert the attention of the brothers from this dream so that they would not get angry with Joseph.

This is why Jacob made it seem like Joseph had dreamed something impossible. After all, Rachel, his mother, had died long ago, which meant it was impossible for her to bow down before him. This means that the rest of the dream had no meaning either. However, the dream did concern Bilha, the maid of Rachel, who raised Joseph after the death of his mother.

We can see that the Torah* equates the foster mother with the real mother, or as our Jewish scholars say: Anyone who takes in an orphan in her house is considered as having given birth to him.

Now a brief word about the war. In the introduction to the verdict of Adolf Eichmann, here in Jerusalem, we can read a summary of the catastrophe which struck the Jewish people in the years of 1940-1945: a chapter full of shed blood and unspeakable suffering which will remain unforgettable in the history of mankind. The other nations, the verdict continues, counted the dead after the war. The Jews counted the survivors.

Here in Yad Vashem, we can empathize somewhat with the atmosphere of that terrible period. You keep wondering when you look at the pictures: How could all this have happened, in broad daylight with so many people involved?

As an answer to this, I will read a press release from the Israeli ambassador to the Netherlands, Mr. E. Ronn, about his speech in 1979 in Utrecht at the presentation of the Yad Vashem awards.

'Millions watched the murder of the Jews. The immense, insane, and incredible murder of Jews was carried out here, in civilized Europe, before our very eyes. Six million times a Jew was murdered, and hundreds of millions watched without lifting a finger. We must not hide the naked truth. Without resignation and without at the very least the passive cooperation of the rulers, governments, and people of Europe, it would not have been possible to murder six million Jews.'

So much for the Israeli ambassador.

We are the psychological and sociological causes of this collective hatred called anti-Semitism*? Which is now called anti-Zionism, anti-Semitism, anti-Israelism? How and with what means can this ancient disease be fought? What lesson should the Jewish people, what lesson should every person learn with respect to his fellow man?

Nine million Dutch people experienced the Second World War, the German occupation. We can count most of you among them. This means that what you see today in Yad Vashem, what you experience here during your holiday in Israel, can be experienced in your own personal way, just like you experienced the war. It has been calculated that between 1939 and 1945 25 million people were murdered in cold blood; people who could not defend themselves: women, men, children, the ill, the elderly, the disabled and babies.

Of these, six million were Jews. Anti-Semitism is not a new concept. For those who are more deeply interested in Jewish history, I recommend reading the book by Werner Keller: 'Diaspora: The Post-Biblical History of the Jews.' This thick pocket edition describes the history of Judaism after the Biblical period up to the present day. I currently do not have the time to go into this further. Germany, where 600,000 Jews lived in the 1930s, was one of the most modern societies at the time. Adolf Hitler became Chancellor and anti-Semitism became part of German state policy. Hitler believed that these German Jews were a threat to the purely Aryan race he wanted. This not only meant a turning point for these German Jews but later also for the eight million Jews elsewhere in Europe. There were already Jews in the Netherlands at the time of the Roman legions. More Jews came to the Netherlands after the First World War. A lot of Jews also came to the Netherlands in the thirties.

Fifty-six years have passed since the Second World War. The event of Jews, deportations, and atrocities in the extermination camps. Other catastrophes have occurred in large parts of the world in these fifty-six years which have partly pushed the Jewish tragedy to the background. Here in Yad Vashem, people continue to work to bring together the archives of the Second World War, which are spread all over the world.

In any case, for us Jews, the years of the Second World War will remain the years of the churban (destruction), the Shoah, the genocide, the disaster, the darkness, the hell, the abyss, the catastrophe, the Holocaust.

The foundation of the Jewish state in 1948 is a confession for the Jewish people in this respect. Death does not have the last word. There is no act of greater holiness than rehabilitation, the restoration of life and human dignity. Throughout the centuries, the Jewish people have responded to their catastrophes in various ways. One of those ways is Yad Vashem. The State of Israel does not have knighthoods and distinctions, like we do in the Netherlands. But what Israel does have that other countries do not, is the Yad Vashem award. The name Yad Vashem comes from Isaiah 56: 5-7.

Weak social groups such as orphans are protected by special laws in the Tanakh*. These enables them to live and work among people. In Isaiah, we read: 'to them I give my house and between my walls A PLACE AND A NAME (Yad Vashem) better than sons and daughters; to each of them I give an eternal name that will never be taken away.'

Yad Vashem certificate of by Mrs. Hennie Rienstra-Oosterkamp, received as a tribute to the Righteous Among the Nations who risked their lives to save Jews during the Holocaust.

The Yad Vashem monument was erected as a reminder, as the national monument for the six million Jewish victims murdered by Nazi Germany during the Second World War. The Avenue of the Righteous, an avenue lined with trees, leads us to the monument. All trees along this avenue and the trees on the Mount of Remembrance have been planted by Gentiles who risked their lives in the Second World War to help Jews escape the Nazi murders. The Righteous of the World. One of those righteous during the war was you, dear mama.

Dear mama, I have now come to the purpose of our gathering. You, mama, will plant a tree in the Avenue of the Righteous Avenue on the Mount of Remembrance. The Commission for the Designation of the Righteous of Yad Vashem announced in December 1980 that they had decided to award you and your late father, Klaas Oosterkamp, the following:

Its highest expression of honor, a medal of honor with the right to plant a tree in the Avenue of the Righteous on the Mount of Remembrance in Jerusalem.

As Isaiah says, this tree planting ceremony will create an eternal monument for you and your family. AN ETERNAL PLACE AND NAME. By planting this tree today, you also erect a monument for my father and mother and for all those many other murdered members of my family who have no grave or gravestone*.

Louis Godschalk

(specific information is based on data available in 1981)

Appendix 7

What will be the new home of this Jewish hidden child?

The battle for Jewish children who ended up hiding at foster families during the war started before the end of the war. They could not go back to their parents if their parents had been murdered. Back to other relatives? Or staying where they are? There are also other motives at play. What about their Jewish identity? Christian people want to help these children but often only if these children receive a Christian education.

A group of resistance fighters met in Amsterdam in the early summer of 1944 to discuss what should happen to the children they had place into hiding. They agreed that any solution needed a legal basis. A committee of five members was formed during this same summer to draw up a bill to this end: Gezina van der Molen, Ger Kempe, An de Waard, Lau Mazirel and Piet Meerburg, all with a legal background.

The Cooperating Underground Child Work Groups wanted to have a strong voice in the future of all Jewish hidden children, not just those saved by themselves but also those they had been placed into hiding by their parents, even if one or both parents would return. They agreed on the allocation of the Jewish orphans to foster parents and absolutely did not consider that the remaining members of the Jewish community would claim these Jewish orphans without parents based on their Jewish background.

In the pre-war Netherlands with its religious segregation, it had been self-evident that the religious communities took care of their orphans and widows. Army rabbi Pereira turned to the Minister of

Justice in London with the urgent request that something should be arranged for these Jewish orphans. He believed that these Jewish children without parents should best be placed *under the temporary guardianship of Jewish institutions*. But the Dutch government considered these Jewish war foster children as a national matter. It feared that the anti-Semitism in the Netherlands after the war would be fed by a separate policy for Jews. They also doubted the capability of the Jewish community to care for these children.

The government also officially recognized the demand by the resistance to have a voice in the decision-making procedure. After all, they have saved the children. If it was clear that the parents of the children were no longer alive, their upbringing and guardianship had to be arranged. The law had to determine where a child would be placed.

There was only one kind of children for the drafters of the bill: the Dutch children. A bill was drawn up which proposed relieving all Jewish parents who had allowed their child to go into hiding from their parental power. They were to demonstrate in the District Court that they were suitable and only then their parental power would be restored. *This was at odds with Dutch family law.*

The guardianship would be in the hands of a state committee called the War Foster Children Guardianship Committee, consisting of child workers. This committee would advise the judge whether the Jewish children could return to their parents or should be left with their (non-Jewish) foster parents.

The committee realized that the deported Jewish parents had suffered and would suffer a lot. This consideration probably led to the following principles:
1. Returning or emerging Jewish parents were expected to be destitute, physically weakened and mentally distressed;
2. The identification of these Jewish parents would be a problem as many will have lost their papers;
3. The identity of many Jewish babies in hiding is unknown;

4. Most Jewish children will now be fully integrated into their (Christian)foster families;
5. Once the Jewish parents emerge or return to Dutch soil, they will not rest until they have found their children. The committee members believed that the Jewish parents could not be blindly reunited with their children.

They derived two arguments in support of the need of a new bill from the above five principles:

A: because of principle 1, the parents cannot be expected to be able to immediately raise their children in a responsible manner. The reunification must at least be postponed until adequate housing is available and it has been determined that they have the mental and physical capacity to properly raise their children.

B: based on the expected passionate search of the Jewish parents, situations in which currently unidentified persons who claim to be the parents obtain the guardianship of children must be avoided. The risk of an inappropriate transfer of parental power is twice as great in case of unidentified children. To avoid this unwanted situation, they considered it wise to leave all Jewish (orphan) children with their foster families for the time being until things were properly arranged. They also expected that they would need to arrange the guardianship for an unknown but large number of Jewish orphans. This resulted in the third argument for the new law.

C: existing legislation assumes that the guardianship of Jewish orphans would be regulated shortly after the death of the parents but *does not provide* for a situation in which a decision can only be taken once the child has already fully integrated into a new family and has become attached to the foster parents.

E: the unanimity on the need to assign children to foster families can be explained by two considerations:

F: the committee members were optimistic about the foster families, which they had partly recruited themselves. They were courageous and had a noble character. The children were housed with good patriots, which would benefit the moral side of their upbringing and the foster families would be rewarded for their courage, if they so wished. The committee members were unaware of the multitude of problems at the foster families.

G: the committee believed that the Jewish children in hiding were mainly Dutch children among other Dutch children. Gezina van der Molen in particular went a long way in this reasoning: the existing legislation provided for allocation within the own religious community. She was an extreme Dutch Calvinist. Now the Jewish children in hiding had changed communities during the war. *They were no longer part of the Jewish segment of society, they were no longer Jewish according to most of the members of the committee.* If they decided to return to their Jewish faith at a later age, they would become Jewish again. She made use of every opportunity to point out the interests of the non-Jewish foster families.

Not all members of the committee agreed with her. Lau Mazirel strongly shared the opinion on Van der Molen; Ger Kempe and An de Waarde had their reservations. But Kempe was arrested that summer, Mazirel was imprisoned for some time, Meerburg and De Waard did attend the meeting. Van der Molen remained alone and with others from her surroundings (J. Donner, J.C. Tenkink and B.W. van Houten) she drew up *the final text of the bill*. The role of Sándor Baracs grew. Mrs. Tellegen from Utrecht and Chief Rabbi J. Tal were consulted as the only non-Trouw employees.

The text of the bill was brought to Eindhoven across the lines on November 21, 1944. However, the text was watered down by the Dutch government in the nine months that followed. The Jewish parents would not be relieved from their parental power but 'suspended'. Sanctions would also be imposed for any failure to comply with the notification requirement. With respect to the Jewish orphans, the decision was made (*in June 1945*) the background and conviction of the deceased parents would be considered when awarding guardianship. It took until August 13, before the law was introduced by Royal Decree.

A few days after the end of the war, on May 8, 1945, the War Foster Children Decree was published in the Government Gazette. The responsibility for the Jewish children was placed in the hands of a committee from the resistance, the Royal Committee for War Foster Children (OPK). Gezina van der Molen became the president and Sándor Baracs the director. The JCC (Jewish Coordination Committee) was founded in Maastricht in January 1945 for the Liberated Dutch Territory, was allowed to nominate Jewish members for the committee to the Minister of Justice and Van der Molen also nominated Jewish members. Some of the Jewish minority who eventually ended up in the committee were very assimilated and voted, at least in the beginning, with the non-Jewish majority. This decision ensured that many Jewish children would stay with their Christian foster families. The remaining Jewish community was sidelined.

The Jewish community did not agree with the decisions. The Jewish guardianship association Le-Ezrath Ha-Jeled* (Help the Child) was founded on August 30, 1945. According to this association, all Jewish orphans had to be placed in a Jewish orphan, without any exceptions.

The registrations flooded in at the OPK offices. In general, the involved parents were reunited with their children as a matter of urgency and without any issues, even though they felt that reunification was extremely difficult in most cases.

There were no signs of any research into the social, physical and mental suitability of the parents. Nor was the identification of the parents an issue. Baracs and his colleagues investigated the identity of unidentified children, the so-called Xs. If they turned out not to be orphans, reunification would take place within a year.

In hindsight, the bill from 1944 bill dealt extensively with irrelevant matters and little with relevant ones. Almost half of the approximately 4,0000 Jewish children who came out of hiding were reunited with one or both parents. Quite a few foster parents gave their child back without involving the OPK.

The actual problem was the allocation of the Jewish orphans. This was the biggest challenge for the OPK and the committee. 2041 Jewish children had become orphans. Conflicts particularly arose of the 1370 orphans who were younger than fifteen years of age. The Jewish minority in the OPK advocated placement in the environment that the parents would have wished. However, the committee rejected membership of a Jewish denomination as simple proof that the parents had desired a Jewish upbringing for their children. This means that a separate decision had to be made for each child and the way to final placement with non-Jewish foster parents was left open. When the children came from clearly Zionist or Orthodox Jewish families, the issues were only minor, and they would be returned to the Jewish environment, with a few notable exceptions. Issues arose concerning Jewish children with more assimilated parents and these would often stay with their foster parents.

The Jewish minority in the committee protested and sometimes received support from unexpected quarters, such as the reformed Rev. J.J. Kalma from Warga in Friesland, who defended the Jewish point of view from his Christian conviction.

The recommendations of the OPK to the District Court reflected only the opinion of the *non-Jewish* majority. The recommendations of the OPK were followed by the District Court, without any research or questions. The Jewish members left the OPK in protest in July 1946. The Minister of Justice set up a committee of inquiry, which agreed with the Jewish opposition on important points. The court had from now on also be informed of the Jewish minority opinion and children of parents who had been contributing members of a Jewish denomination on 9 May 1940 had to be raised in a Jewish environment unless there were compelling reasons against this. Tensions quickly rose again after that as the OPK let the interests, and their anti-Jewish opinion be the decisive factor again.

The Minister dissolved the OPK and transferred the remaining cases to the Child Protection Board in Amsterdam in July 1949. The number of children that was assigned to non-Jewish foster parents fell dramatically after this. Of the approximately 1370 orphans under 15 years of age, 358 remained in a non-Jewish environment, more than a quarter of the total for which the OPK originally was to give an opinion. The others were taken in by Jewish families and a number of orphans were placed in Jewish orphanages.

Literature:

- Flim, Bert Jan. Omdat hun hart sprak. Geschiedenis van de georganiseerde hulp aan Joodse kinderen in Nederland.
- Citroen, Michal. U wordt door niemand verwacht. Nederlandse joden na kampen en onderduik.
- Drs. Evers-Emden, Bloeme. Geschonden bestaan.

Appendix 8

Genealogy of the Godschalk and Zwaaf families

My father: Lion Godschalk, born on 14-07-1916 in Amsterdam
My mother: Anna Zwaaf, born on 22-09-1917 in Amsterdam.
                  Married on 05-06-1940
My sister: Cornelia, born on 31-08-41, died at home on 03-01-1942
Louis: Born, 1-11-1942

Grandfather: Louis Godschalk, born on 05-08-1888 in Amsterdam
Grandmother: Cornelia Jacobs, born on 15-03-1891 in Amsterdam
                  Father, mother and grandparents deported on 20-07-1943, murdered in Sobibor on 23-07-1943

Grandfather: Hartog Zwaaf, born on 20-10-1885 in Amsterdam
Grandmother: Clara Zwaaf-Zwaaf, born on 29-04-1884 in Breda
                  Grandparents deported on 23-10-1942, murdered in Auschwitz* on 26-10-1942

Aunt: Hendrika Godschalk, born on 02-03-1914 in Amsterdam
                  Married to: Hartog de Hoop, born on 09-11-1910 in Königssteele, Germany
                  Son: Louis, born on 05-09-1940
                  As a family deported on 18-05-1943, murdered in Sobibor on 21-05-1943

Aunt: Lena Zwaaf, born on 17-03-1925 in Amsterdam
                  Murdered in Sobibor on 21-05-1943

Uncle:	Levi Zwaaf, born on 30-01-1913 in Amsterdam
Murdered in Auschwitz on 03-10-1944
Married to: Rachel Aldewereld, born on 02-04-1915 in Amsterdam
Son: Isaac Zwaaf, born on 25-03-1938
Aunt Rachel and nephew Hartog-Isaac, murdered in Auschwitz on 08-10-1942
Uncle:	Simon Zwaaf, born on 10-06-1910 in Amsterdam
Murdered in External Command Trawniki on 30-11-1943

Married to: Ester Zwaaf -van Beem, born on 12-10-1913
Daughter: Clara Zwaaf, born on 01-02-1936
Aunt Ester and niece Clara, murdered in Sobibor on 14-05-1943 |
| Parents of Ester: | Jonas van Beem, born on 07-03-1888 in Amsterdam
Judith Brandon, born on 08-03-1888 in Amsterdam
Both murdered in Auschwitz on 14-09-1942 |
| Brother of Ester: | David van Beem, born on 17-3-1917 in Amsterdam
Murdered in Auschwitz on 30-09-1942

Married to: Sara Sealtiel, born on 17-1-1918 in Amsterdam
Son: Jonas, born on 06-08-1940
Sara and Janos were murdered in Auschwitz on 23-07-1942 |

Appendix 9

Max Abram

It is early 1941 when the parents of Max Abram, Abraham Abram and Hadasse Abram, go into hiding in Bussum with their daughter Ans (born on 26 February 1933) and their son Max (born on November 20, 1934). Max goes to school in Baarn.

Mrs. Abram is arrested by the Germans during a raid and ends up in camp Fal Liebau and does not survive the war. At the beginning of 1944 and after ten different hiding addresses, Max arrives at Mr. and Mrs. Abma, who ran one of the four bakeries in Scharnegoutum, a village 3 km from Sneek. The policeman Sikke de Jong has helped to find this hiding address. This will be the eleventh hiding address for Max, 9 years old, his hair that has been colored blonde. It will be his last. He receives a false identity document with the name Jan Dekker. Max did not go into hiding with the Abma family, he is supposedly an evacuee. The Abma family has 2 children: Aagje and Hilbrand. Max goes to primary school in Scharnegoutum under the name Jan Dekker. He helps in the bakery and sells bread. I arrive at my last hiding address in Scharnegoutum on April 14, 1944. I am 18 months old then and Max is 9.

At the end of the end of the fifties, Hennie Oosterkamp, my foster mother at that time, tells me she has informed Jan Dekker (Max) that she was caring for a Jewish child. When Max past the Factory Houses in Scharnegoutum with his cargo bike with bread, he greets me. Mr. Abma taught Max to swim and later did the same for me. Mr. Abma swam almost all year round at the same place in the Zwette, near the grass drying facility in Scharnegoutum, close to the cow dairy plant of my school friend Joop Koopmans. A large, empty cookie tin was tied to your back to stay afloat and that is how you went into the water.

Max has a driving license and a car in the early fifties. He regularly visits the Abma family. I am sometimes invited to the communal lunch. In this period, I annually stay in Amsterdam with the Cosman family in the Albert Cuypstraat in Amsterdam. I would visit Max and his father, who had a wholesale business in women's and men's clothing in the Albert Cuypstraat.

When Max is eighteen years old, he starts trading in scarves, buttons and the like with a limited exemption from the subdistrict court (as he was not yet 21). When he is 27, Max buys a store building in the Jordaan, purchases fabrics and has them turned into ladies' coats by a workshop. This is in 1961: the start of Clothing Company Max Abram at Karthuizersdwarsstraat 27 in Amsterdam. When this building becomes too small, he moves the company to the Prinsengracht. An enormous building at Prinseneiland in Amsterdam is bought in 1965. His last move is to a state-of-the-art building at the Basisweg in Amsterdam.

At the start of 1964, Max and his business partner Herman van Ree open a ladies' coat store in Hilversum called 'Het Mantelhuis in de Leeuwenstraat'. The mother-in-law of Mr. van Ree, Stella Dresden, manages this store. Max opens a 'Mantelhuis' in Rotterdam in 1964. A Mantelhuis also opens in The Hague in that same year. Coats are sold in sizes from 38 to 56 at prices ranging from fl. 59.00 and 69.00. The first store in Belgium opens in 1976 and Germany follows in 1983. The name later changes to Mantelspecialist, later abbreviated to M&S Mode.

Max marries Betty Cosman in 1964. Two children are born: Linda Hadasse (1966) and Richard Max (1968). Linda moves to America in 1984 and Richard to Thailand in 1998. When I wanted to open my third Mantelhuis in Groningen in 1967, the owners of the store demanded a security because I had a young business which was not yet financially strong. Betty provided this security for me. Max sells his company, consisting of 150 M&S fashion stores and 20 lingerie stores, to De Bijenkorf in 1987. He has already sold 20 Nelemans stores, discount fashion stores, to Anton Dreesmann.

Max has his offices and home in the Viottastraat since 1993, where once the villa of Florrie, the widow of NSB* leader Meinoud Rost van Tonningen. Max has a skybox in the Arena. When I am in Amsterdam and Ajax plays a home match, he gives me a chance to go with him. Even more important for Max is his bridge hobby. Max and his friend Herman van Drenkelford together have a bridge club in Zeist: The White House.

When Ajax plays during a bridge match, Max chooses to play bridge. Max plays bridge at the second highest level in the First Division. Max believes that business and bridge are communicating vessels. Whoever can play the 'game' best, wins!

Appendix 10

Jacques Grishaver

Jacques Grishaver was born on March 20, 1942. His parents and he survived the Second World War with the help of the resistance, but his family members were murdered. Jacques remembers that he and his father sometimes hid in a cupboard.

With Loe Lap as his great example, Jacques and his wife Loes had an army dump shop in the Eerste van Swindenstraat in Amsterdam. Jacques and his wife joined the Liberal Jewish Congregation (LJG) in Amsterdam in 1984. Jacques was interim director of this LJG for some time in the eighties. He and Loes decided to sign up for the Poland trip organized by the Dutch Auschwitz Committee in 1989. He mainly wanted to visit Sobibor. 'I wanted to stand on the same platform of the station where the cattle wagons delivered Jews from Westerbork to be murdered on that *same* day.'

Sobibor is the place where my Jewish family members experienced the last, most anxious moments of their life on Earth. 'I became afraid shortly before the planned trip, I was not emotionally ready yet. I was still sick of the war and my psychologist advised me not to go. Loes and I did manage to go on the Poland trip, organized by the Dutch Auschwitz Committee, the next year.'

Jacques has experienced long periods of illness a number of times, which were inextricably linked to the Shoah. Jacques and Loes have two children, Angelique and Mischa, and four grandchildren. Jacques has been involved in the NAC as a volunteer since 1989. He is the chairman of this committee since 1998.

The NAC annually organizes:
- The 'National Holocaust Remembrance', which was acknowledged by the Dutch government in 2012;
- The annual 'Never Again Auschwitz Lecture';
- Group trips to the extermination camps in Poland.

On December 16, 2016, the NAC created, together with the Polish-Jewish architect Daniel Libeskind, the design for the Dutch National Monument to the Holocaust. This national monument will be located in the heart of the Jewish Quarter of Amsterdam where it all happened more than seventy years ago. It will be the first Dutch memorial with the names of all 102,000 Jews and 220 Roma and Sinti who were murdered during the Second World War. It will be located in the Weesperstraat, close to the Hermitage Museum and the Protestant Diaconate, not far from major Jewish cultural institutions such as the Portuguese Synagogue and the Jewish Historical Museum.

Jacques was appointed 'Knight of the Order of Orange-Nassau' by the Queen for his years of volunteering for the NAC.

Appendix 11

Memories of Nida and Louis Blok-Blitz

Southport, 27 Dec. 1992

Dear Louis and Ivonne,
 Thank you for your letter of December 10, 1992 and your well wishes for us for the year 1993. We hope that it will also be a prosperous year for you, which will not only bring prosperity but also health to your family. Your request to tell you something about what I can remember about your father and family immediately made me think. Once I started thinking about it, it was a bit difficult as it has been years and since we are now living in a completely different environment the past fades away much more quickly. However, I will do my best and hope to tell you things that you do not know yourself.

To be honest, I am not even sure what you know about your parents and how you ended up with your foster parents. We will start with the Godschalk family. First your grandfather Louis Godschalk (he was called Lowietje), who was married to Kee, whose maiden name I have forgotten. They had drugstore in the Linnaeusstraat in Amsterdam and also sold paint. It was a busy store. They were nice, proper people, always in for a joke. Uncle Lowietje could tell jokes or get up unexpectedly, make a trumpet of his hands, and march around the table to his homemade marching music until everyone in the room followed him and we all had a lot of fun. I often stayed with them and was well cared for while they made sure I ate enough, as I did not do so at home. Rika, the older sister of your father, also paid a lot of attention to me.

Your father married a few years later. Your mother was a handsome girl, a nice fine and a slim figure. I cannot tell whether you look like him from the picture you sent us, your face is hidden behind a beard. The parents of your mother had a delicatessen shop in the Jodenbreestraat. Your father was, just like mine, a painter by profession and took over the store from your grandparents after his marriage. He lived above the store with your mother. He had studied to become an accountant. I can remember that he visited us on a Tuesday afternoon in the Van Wouwstraat, where my parents had a drapery shop, and taught me to ride on his men's bike, which was not easy of course. He was around 14-15 years old then. He also liked to tease. His sister Rika was often the target, not me.

When he was around 7 years old and I was about 5 years old, he visited us with his mother in The Hague, where I lived most of my years as a girl. We lived in Amsterdam from my 1st to my 12th year. During at least one of their visits to The Hague we were in our backyard and he scared me. By digging up large, fat worms. He often asked me if I remembered that years later. The sister of your father, Rika, married in about 1936 to Hartog de Hoop, who worked as a butcher, and later did the same as your grandfather and opened a drugstore.

We lived in The Hague and moved to Voorschoten, near Leiden, a few years later to live with my parents. Not a lot of Jewish people lived in Voorschoten and it is much calmer than in a large city. More than a year later, we were summoned to move to Germany, supposedly to work. My husband first made sure that my parents could go into hiding with clients of his in Naaldwijk. We then went to Groningen to try to go to England by boat. This turned out to be impossible. We briefly went into hiding in Leiden and then decided to leave the country by land. We first went to Amsterdam, where we only found Rika, who was alone with her one-year old son as her husband was away at that time. We suggested that she left Holland with us, but she did not dare to attempt this with a small child. If she were to be summoned to go to Germany, she assumed it would only be to work.

We travelled to Brabant and went into hiding at a farm for a short time (about 2 weeks), which time we used to prepare our escape across the border. We travelled by train to Spain through Belgium, unoccupied and occupied France. We crossed the borders on foot, which took three to four days in the Pyrenees, where we were ultimately arrested. My husband ended up in a camp where he spent seven months and I spent two weeks in prison because we were illegal. I was brought to Madrid, where I was housed in a hotel until my husband was released from the camp.

The Dutch consulate in Madrid wanted to send us to Curaçao but we wanted to go to Palestine. We went to Portugal on our own and received permission from the Representative of the Dutch Government to take a special boat to Palestine at the expense of the government on condition that we would take care of ourselves there. When we arrived in Palestine everyone on the boat was put into a 'camp' by the English and subjected to a thorough investigation. It was wartime and the English had published a 'Whitepaper' in 1939 to restrict Jewish immigration. We were among the first group to be released and there were buses in front of the camp which would take us to Haifa or Jerusalem for free. We chose for Tel Aviv but did not have a real preference as there would be possibilities everywhere. We were waiting for the departure and a man approached us and asked if there were any Dutch people. We were the only ones and he asked us why we wanted to go to Tel Aviv. He came from a kibbutz north of Haifa and wanted to take us there to shelter us for the time being and introduce us to the Dutch colony. We were fine with this and that is how our stay in Haifa began.

In January 1946, we came back to Holland from Palestine by the first cargo boat that transported oranges to Holland. We found my parents who had survived the war healthy and well. They had spent about 3 years in an attic and were very happy with their granddaughter. We moved to Voorschoten again where we were visited by a great-cousin of my mother, Jet Duveen. She told us that Lion's and Anna's baby had to be somewhere, who had been given to the resistance by his parents with the request to take care of him. We found an address of an institution in Amsterdam and I visited it. We were shown a picture of a boy I recognized immediately: he looked exactly like Lion. The man asked if I was absolutely certain and asked me for the names of the parents and grandparents.

We knew where you were and visited you there. And then the big problem arose. We were convinced that your parents would have wanted you to grow up in a Jewish environment. We were also convinced that taking you away from foster parents would cause them great sadness. This brings us to your questions about that conference in the RAI. Yes, it was indeed difficult to get children back to the Jewish environment. We are convinced that the foster parents, who had stood up as the actual parents, were more highly valued by the judge than the remaining family members who wanted to bring the child back into Jewish family life. Your foster mother, Hennie, had risked her life when the life of the child was in danger. We were not completely certain that we had the right to cause your foster mother grief by taking you away from her. Was being Jewish enough to disturb the family life you had been experiencing for 5 to 6 years? What could be the consequences for this child when he would be taken from his familiar surroundings and assigned to Jewish relatives who were strangers to him?

We left it to the judge to consider the interests and accepted the ruling. There was an option to appeal against this. But we were advised not to do so because experience had shown that this was generally not successful. We also thought it was better to leave it at the discretion of the judge. The Jewish environment took care of itself in the end. You started looking for your Jewish identity yourself without external influences based on your own feelings and now live in Israel with your family. We have later given you a book with our name and address on one of the first pages. We hoped that you would later feel the need to connect with us once you had grown up. That had to be possible.

We asked your foster parents if you could come and visit us or stay with us during school holidays to get to know us as a family. They rejected our request, much to our regret. Jet Duveen later told us that you would stay with her every once in a while, to which we responded that our request had been rejected. She promised to keep us informed. Once you came to Amsterdam again, she would let us know and we could come as well so you could meet us and our daughters. We do not know why but all her good intentions never materialized. We made a special trip to Amsterdam one time to remind her of her promise and received the same promise but never heard a word from her again.

We hope that this letter tells you about some matters and facts you were not aware of. As I said at the beginning, I am not sure how much you have figured out yourself already. I hope that you can let me know whether this information is of any value to you and if you want to learn more about some things. I hope I can be of service to you again.

Warm regards from us both (*Nida and Louis Blok Blitz*), also from our daughters and their families, for Ivonne, you, and your two children.

Appendix 12

Simon Meerschwam

I visited the autumn fashion fair in the RAI in Amsterdam in the autumn of 1974. On the way to the exit, a man approached me with a smile. He held out his hand and said: 'Let me introduce myself, I am Simon Meerschwam'. He asked me if I had seen the fashion items sold by Kolbo 2001. I said: 'Yes.' When he asked me if I had bought anything, I said 'no.' He asked why not, and I responded: 'Your prices are equal to or higher than the prices for which I sell this type of lady fashion articles, your seller does not want to adjust the price based on the numbers I need for my fashion stores.'

(*Discounts were only given for large quantities as bought by fashion groups like C&A, V&D or Miss Etam*).

Mr. Meerschwam gave me an understanding and asked me if I had lunch yet. Before I could answer, he looked at me with a smile and said: 'I have kosher* sandwiches, come have one with me as I want to discuss something with you.' He told me that he understood my price problem with Kolbo 2001 but that his son would take over the women's fashion wholesale activities in the Confectiecentrum in Amsterdam in a couple of months and that Jack would definitely find a way to do business together. According to his father, Jack was a first-class young fashion buyer who could sell the desired quantities at the for me desired prices.

Mr. Meerschwam was a successful businessman himself. He had a very successful menswear wholesaler in the Confectiecentrum in Amsterdam. We had a long talk. I never have long conversations at fashion fairs as I simply do not have the time, but this was a very special and unique personality. We have a click form the moment when he mentioned 'kosher' sandwiches. Mr. Meerschwam' knew that I was Jewish without asking anything. We were 'mishpokhe' from that moment. He invited me to visit his showroom for a cup of coffee, to stay in touch with him until Jack returned from America, who would then become my point of contact.

Jack started a few months later and just as Mr. Meerschwam had predicted, I could buy unlimited quantities from Kolbo 2001. Mr. Meerschwam was right, Jack bought the right fashion items at the right time and the purchase prices were never a problem. Ivonne and I became friends with the whole Meerschwam family.

Charlotte and Simon had an apartment in Jerusalem. When Simon went too far away countries to buy products, Charlotte did not want to stay at home alone and went to her apartment in Jerusalem. She would often call Ivonne there. They could talk to each other for hours.

Simon Meerschwam, born on November 22, 1915, had a heart attack in 2002 during his stay with his family in Eilat for Pesach and fell into a coma. He passed away on April 22, 2002. Out of respect for what Mr. Meerschwam meant to me, I flew to Amsterdam to attend the lewaja (Jewish funeral) and the shiva*.

Charlotte Meerschwam, born on September 8, 1920, died on October 7, 2004. Ivonne and I were in Amsterdam, so I could also attend her lewaja.

'May their souls be part of the bundle of eternal life.'

Names and definitions

Aliyah
Is the immigration of Jews from the diaspora to the Land of Israel. Also defined as 'the act of going up' or 'ascent' – that is, towards Jerusalem – 'making Aliyah' by moving to the Land of Israel is one of the most basic tenets of Zionism. In the rabbinic tradition, the country of Israel is spiritually considered spiritually the highest point of the world. In this tradition, the land of Israel also represents the highest spiritual values in the world. The State of Israel's Law of Return gives Jews and their descendants automatic rights regarding residency and Israeli citizenship. The large-scale immigration of Jews to Palestine began in 1882. Since the establishment of the State of Israel in 1948, more than 3 million Jews have moved to Israel. Return to the land of Israel is a recurring theme in Jewish prayers recited every day, three times a day, and Jewish Holiday services on Passover and Yom Kippur traditionally conclude with the words 'Next year in Jerusalem'. Because Jewish lineage can provide a right to Israeli citizenship.
Aliyah (returning to Israel) has both a secular and a religious significance. When a person is called up to Reading of the Torah (this is also called Aliyah).

Amen
The word first occurs in the Hebrew Bible in Numbers 5:22 when the Priest addresses a suspected adulteress and she responds 'Amen, Amen'. Overall, the word appears in the Hebrew Bible 30 times. Whenever one hears another recite a blessing he should answer 'Amen' at its conclusion. The 'Amen' constitutes an 'endorsement', and affirmation that the blessing is true.

Anti-Semitism
Is hostility to, prejudice, or discrimination against Jews. To hate Jews. This has existed hundreds of years before the calendar in Alexandria. There was already a venomous and violent anti-Semitism before the birth of Christianity. Christianity has added the murder of Jesus. Jews were a minority in all countries where they lived from 73 to 1948. This made them vulnerable and dependent on the good will of the majority over the centuries. This good will is sometimes absent or insufficient, which results in hatred or discrimination against Jews, orally, in writing, in regulations, or with physical or verbal violence. This is called anti-Semitism. Anti-Semitism is often accompanied by prejudice. Prejudices and stereotypes that are untrue but persistent. This hatred and prejudice are expressed in a variety of ways. The most serious and gruesome things that have occurred over the centuries: considering Jews as second-class citizens of a country, removing Jews from society, and the structural extermination of Jews in a country, city, or region. The word 'anti-Semitism' originated in the nineteenth century as a euphemistic scientific term for hatred of Jews. Because there is no such thing as 'semitism', it is quite pointless to describe the word 'anti-Semitism' as anti-Semitism. The anti-Semitic stories are all one hundred percent nonsense. The monotheistic culture of Judaism and Christianity clashed with Greek and Roman culture because monotheism claims absolute truth. This guarantees intolerance and conflict.

Auschwitz
Auschwitz concentration camp was a network of concentration and extermination camps built and operated by Nazi Germany in occupied Poland during World War II. It consisted of Auschwitz I (the original concentration camp), Auschwitz II–Birkenau (a combined concentration/extermination camp), Auschwitz III–Monowitz (a labour camp to staff an IG Farben factory), and 45 satellite camp. The first extermination of prisoners took place in September 1941. Auschwitz II–Birkenau went on to become a major site of the Nazis' Final Solution to the Jewish Question during the Holocaust. From early 1942 until late 1944, transport trains delivered Jews to the camp's

gas chambers from all over German-occupied Europe, where they were murdered en masse with the cyanide-based poison Zyklon B, originally developed to be used as a pesticide. An estimated 1.3 million people were sent to the camp, of whom at least 1.1 million were murdered. Around 90 percent of those were Jews. Auschwitz was a place with ten thousand inhabitants until 1940. In 1944, two hundred thousand people lived in the city of Oswiecim for the enormous industrial area, fish ponds, greenhouses, wheat fields and the like. The 'employees' were forced Jewish laborers from the nearby 'camp'. Auschwitz is globally known as an extermination camp. However, the camps were mainly set up as labor camps at the start of the Hitler regime. It was how Hitler repaid the German industry that had brought him to power. He provided it with cheap Jewish labor as a form of thanks. It is not entirely correct to attribute the murder of the Jews in Auschwitz to only 'racial ideology'.

Baracs

The Hungarian Jew Sándor Baracs (1900-2002) was given the opportunity by a former German employer to settle in the Netherlands in 1927. He was naturalized and settled in Amsterdam as an importer of Hungarian fruit juices. Baracs was one of the few who started with his resistance at the beginning of the war under the name Uncle Piet. He became active in a small armed resistance group in 1940. He was in danger, went into hiding in September 1942, was given false papers, all without giving up his work for the resistance. He was a fried of the Boissevain family. He got in touch with Mrs. Boissevain sister, Hester van Lennep, who had a skin care institute near his hiding place. She and her assistant sometimes had Jewish mothers with children in their institute. She not only bleached the hair of the children at the request of the mothers, she also did their best to house these Jewish children at family or friends. The non-religious Jewish man and young woman from an old and respected reformed lineage not only worked together in the resistance, they also fell in love for life. They managed to get married during the war in 1944. The assimilated and mixed married *(baptized, according to some)* Jewish businessman became the director of the OPK Offices and a member of the daily management. Baracs once introduced himself to someone. This person said: 'Baracs? Have you ever been the director of the OPK?' Baracs said 'Yes sir'. He was told: 'Then you are the most hated man in the Netherlands'.

Bar Mitzvah
When a boy reaches his religious majority upon reaching the age anniversary of his thirteen birthday according to the Hebrew calendar. From then on, as an adult, he is required to comply with the Jewish regulations (mitzvot). This is called 'Bar Mitzvah', subject of the commandment. He will be called to the Torah for the first time to read from it himself. The Bar Mitzvah boy has prepared for this for a long time, it is a piece of text with difficult words in Hebrew and without vowels that he reads out at a certain melody. Reaching Bar Mitzvah and Bat Mitzvah is accompanied by a festive celebration. Bar Mitzvah and Bat Mitzvah: under Jewish law, a boys and girls become liable for his action once he/she turns thirteen/twelve years old.

Bat Mitzvah
A girl is called 'Bat Mitzvah', 'daughter of the commandment'. This happens when she turns twelve according to the Hebrew calendar. In Judaism, Bar Mitzvah and Bat Mitzvah are an initiation, a ceremony, to be included in the covenant G'd made with patriarch Abraham. She will from that moment be required to comply with the mitzvot.

Beth Din
This is a Rabbinic court (highly educated prominent rabbis) where people take oral exams to demonstrate that they have sufficient knowledge of Judaism. We chose to become a member of the Conservative/Masority Synagogue in Ra'anana in the early eighties. If Lion Patrick wanted to do Bar Mitzvah in this synagogue, we had to 'come out' as a family in accordance with the requirements of this synagogue. The chairman of this synagogue has taught Lion Patrick for over a year to ensure he could lead the service during his Bar Mitzvah in the synagogue during the Sabbath. This was a difficult task when it came to text and melodies. He did it out of respect and on behalf for our Jewish family, who were almost completely exterminated.

Rabbi Dov Vogel come to our home every Thursday evening for a year teaching Judaism to the whole family . He went with us to the Beth Din of the Conservative synagogue in Jerusalem. Ivonne (Osnat), Anna Vanessa (Channa), and Lion Patrick (Arjeh) were examined about their knowledge there. The Beth Din ruled positively. All three received a document. A chuppah was then realized for Osnat Bat Ya'acov (Ivonne's Jewish name) and Ben Zion (Louis's Jewish name) on the spot.

Under Orthodox Jewish law, 'coming out and meeting the requirements of the *Conservative* synagogue' is not enough. Anna Vanessa and Lion Patrick wished to officially come out according to the *orthodox* requirements after that. Anna Vanessa took the orthodox Beth Din exam on a day Ivonne and I could not attend. I accompanied Lion Patrick to the Orthodox Beth Din. Without knowing in advance, I was also called to appear before the Beth Din.

The highly learned and experienced rabbis of the Orthodox Beth Din said they only wanted to get acquainted with me, as father of Lion Patrick. After the introduction, a stream of questions came. It was not easy for me to answer the barrage of still, for me, difficult questions. Questions about the Torah, Rabbinic writings, Jewish Holidays, synagogue service, Jewish world history, often used Jewish terminology, and so on. Difficult, even though I had learned a lot from Mr. Cohen in Leeuwarden, studied more than ten years with Rabbi Dasberg, one year with rabbi Dov Vogel, one and a half years in the Israeli guide school and having read and studied at home bookcases full of Jewish literature.

Anna Vanessa and Lion Patrick received the rabbinical document stating that they are now officially included in the Jewish people.

B"H
B'ezrat HaShem ('with G'ds help'), also read as Baruch HaShem ('Thank G'd').

Boot Ids
Ids Boot (his Jewish name was David Willem Vischjager (1943-2004) from Sneek went to the MULO in Sneek in the same time as me. We lost track of each other when I moved to Leeuwarden. We were surprised to see each other again at the conference 'The Hidden Children' in Amsterdam. During this schooltime we both were not aware of our Jewish roots. Now in 1992 our life stories were swapped in bits and pieces. Besides all similarities, there were enormous differences. Ids was also smuggled out of the nursery. While my parents, on the advice of Walter Susskind, made the heroic decision to let me be saved by child rescuers, David Willem Vischjager his mother had taken many risks with him. She was in hiding herself and did not prevent her only child from being moved around until he was ultimately brought, to the nursery across The Hollandsche Schouwburg, in Amsterdam by a family member. He was, like me, ill and malnourished when he was taken to Sneek in November 1943 and housed with the family of Jelte Boot and Hotske Hospes. Jelte was municipal worker and a member of the resistance. The fact that David Willem Vischjager participated in The Hidden Children conference indicated that his Jewish root eventually pulled on him as well. We agreed to keep in touch.

Bounty hunters
Dutch collaborationist were used to track down Jews in hiding in 1943. They received 7.50 guilders (*kopgeld*) for each Jew in hiding they managed to arrest.

Brit Milah
'Covenant of circumcision'; is a Jewish religious male circumcision ceremony performed by a mohel ('circumciser') – A mohel is a Jew trained in the practice of *brit milah*, the 'covenant of circumcision' – on the eighth day of the infant's life. The *brit milah* is followed by a celebratory meal. According to the Hebrew Bible (Genesis 17:10-14) God commanded the Biblical patriarch Abraham to be circumcised, an act to be followed by his descendants.

CADSU
The German word Wiedergutmachung after World War II refers to the reparations that the German government agreed to pay in 1953 to the direct survivors of the Holocaust, and to those who were made to work as forced labour or who otherwise became victims of the Nazis. The noun Wiedergutmachung is the general term for 'restitution' or 'reparation'. The noun is made up of wieder ('again'), gut('good' or 'well'), and machung, a verbal noun of machen ('to make'). The verb wiedergutmachen means literally 'to make good again' or to compensate The Central Settlement Office for German Claims for Compensation, abbreviated to CADSU in Dutch.

C&A
Kai Bosecker: https://www.vn.nl/ca-zuiver-arisch-in-de-oorlog (Dutch)

Chuppah
A chuppah literally, 'canopy' or 'covering'), is a canopy under which a Jewish couple stand during their wedding ceremony. I placed inside the synagogue or outside under the star-filled sky. This is because people will be able to see the sky directly above the chuppah, which reminds them of the Biblical promise that the descendants of Patriarch Abraham will multiply like the stars in heaven. It consists of a cloth or sheet, sometimes a tallit – in Judaism, a tallite or talles is a rectangular bordered prayer carpet with wires on the four corners, called tzitzit, worn by men during the morning prayer – stretched or supported over four poles, or sometimes manually held up by attendants to the ceremony. A chuppah symbolizes the home that the couple will build together.

Cosman
Bettie and Sam. After my mother Anna Zwaaf was born in 1917, my grandparents decided to look for a girl to take care after Anna day and night to ensure my grandmother could continue working in their stores. This nanny was Bettie. Bettie met Sam Cosman in the Zwaaf residence. Seven years later Bettie and Sam told my grandmother that they were planning to get married. My grandmother did not want to

let Bettie go. She insisted that Bettie would continue to take care of her daughter Anna until she became an adult. My mother also wanted to stay with Bettie. As a solution, the couple agreed to take Anna to Belgium, where Sam got a job in the diamond industry. Anna later met Lion Godschalk at a Jewish High Holiday dance party in Belgium. It went well, and they felt a spark. The two became a couple and not just on the dance floor. After their chuppah, they continued the family business in Amsterdam with Lion his parents. After the war, Bettie and Sam looked for relatives of Sam and survivors of the Godschalk and Zwaaf families. This is how they found me.

El Malé Rachamiem
A prayer asking for peace of the souls of victims of anti-Semitism. Jews have had to endure persecution throughout the centuries. The El Malé Rachamiem was written for the martyrs of the Middle Ages. The names of some concentration and extermination camps are mentioned in the version after the Second World War. To say this prayer, a minyan (ten Jewish men) must be present, just like for the kaddish.

Giyur
Judaism is not a faith that seeks to convert people. You can become Jewish. This is an often difficult, far-reaching and lengthy process. Only a few people become Jewish. Giyur means conversion to Judaism. Admission to Judaism is not an easy matter. Even when you have a Jewish father and an extremely positive mother who creates a Jewish atmosphere at home and a kosher* household.

Judaism is a tolerant religion, which means that Jews do *not* believe that Judaism is the only, the best and the only universal religion. Each person with whatever philosophy of life (not only religious) is equal and is tasked with making the world a better place. Judaism is not a *conversion* religion, unlike Christianity and Islam for example. You can become Jewish, even if you were not born a Jew. But only if you have genuine intentions and are willing to devote a lot of time, energy, study, actions and change your entire lifestyle. Judaism is more of an *action* religion than a (passive) *faith* religion.

In order to determine whether Judaism is his or her destiny, a person must:
- be familiar with the course of events during a synagogue service;
- study Judaism and its history of Judaism;
- learn the melodies used during the synagogue service;
- learn the Jewish rites for home and put them into practice and follow them;
- keep a home with the laws of Kashrut*,
- celebrate Shabbat and Jewish Holidays;
- (sometimes) be adopted by an Orthodox Jewish family to learn all customs;
- learn the texts Torah and Rabbinic writings;
- be familiar with the Jewish life cycle;
- know the Jewish history;
- understand the Jewish world;
- know commonly used Jewish terminology;
- and a lot more.

The teacher determines when the oral exam will be taken by a Beth Din. This is a Rabbinic court that assesses whether someone has sufficient knowledge of Judaism.

Godschalk
Godschalck, Godeschalk and the German variants Gottschalk and Gottschal; also Gosschalk and the Flemish Godschalx and Goetschalckx. All these names have the first name of Godschalk, derived from 'God' and 'schalk', which last word originally meant 'servant'; the complete name meant 'G-d's servant'. It already appeared in pre-Christian times, 'God' referring to a pagan god. It also became a Christian name mainly used by clergymen.
Godschalk: from: http://familiegodschalk.nl/genealogie/index.html (Dutch)

Gravestone
'May his/her soul be part of the bundle of eternal life'. The bottom of an obituary and a gravestone often contain the Hebrew letters T.N.Tz.B.H. This abbreviation means: Tehee nafsjo/nafsjà tseroera

bitsror hachajiem – may his/her soul be part of the bundle of eternal life – The source of this wish is I Samuel 25:29 where Abigail says to David: 'May a person stand up to persecute and hate you, then the soul of my lord will be bound in the bundle of the living at the Eternal your G'd – wehajeta nefesj adonie tseroera bitsror hachajiem...' (See gravestone*)

Hanukah
Literally 'dedication' is a Jewish holiday commemorating the rededication of the Second Temple in Jerusalem at the time of the Maccabean Revolt. A Jewish rebellion, lasting from 167 to 160 BC, led by the Maccabees against the Seleucid Empire and the Hellenistic influence on Jewish life. Hanukah is observed for eight nights and days, starting on the 25th day of Kislev according to the Hebrew calendar, which may occur at any time from late November to late December in the Gregorian calendar. It is also known as the Festival of Lights and the Feast of Dedication. The festival is observed by lighting the candles of a candelabrum with nine branches, called a Hanukah menorah (or hanukkiah). One branch is typically placed above or below the others and its candle is used to light the other eight candles. This unique candle is called the *shamash* (Hebrew: for 'attendant'). Each night, one additional candle is lit by the *shamash* until all eight candles are lit together on the final evening of the Holiday. Other Hanukah festivities include playing dreidel and eating oil-based foods such as doughnuts and latkes. Since the 1970s, the worldwide Chabad Hasidic movement has initiated public hanukkiah lightings in open public places in many countries.

JMW
Joods Maatschappelijk Werk (Jewish Social Work). This is the national welfare organization for the Jewish community in the Netherlands. Its activities have been divided into three sectors: Aid, Home Care and Jewish activities. JMW offers psychosocial aid, home care, socio-cultural activities and care to young people, adults and the elderly from its head offices in Amsterdam and several regional offices.

JNF
The Jewish National Fund Netherlands was founded in May 1902 and is one of the oldest fundraising organizations in the Netherlands. The goal of the fund is to develop the State of Israel and make it inhabitable for all its inhabitants. The Jewish National Fund focuses on the development of sustainable, ecological projects for the benefit of the quality of life of all people in Israeli society. The JNF focuses in particular on afforestation, agriculture and horticulture, innovative water management and research.

Jews
Jews with a capital letter, not with a small 'j'. The words Jews and Jewish were written with a capital letter before the Second World War. The Nazis decreed that a small 'j' must be used for Jew and all words and terms derived from it. It is an anti-Semitic creep in our Dutch spelling used to this date. I write everything that contains the word Jew, including all words and terms derived from it, with a capital letter out of respect.

JOKOS
Stichting Joodse Kerkgenootschappen en Sociale Organisaties in Nederland voor Schadevergoedingsaangelegenheden (Jewish Church Organizations and Social Organizations in the Netherlands for Damage Claim Matters). This is a collaboration of a number of Jewish organizations. After the war, this foundation submitted a claim to the Federal Republic of Germany for compensation of looted household effects. The looting of these households was called M-Aktion (Möbel-Aktion), which is why the claims were called Möbel claims or M-Claims. The files do not contain any personal documents but only documents related to the claim such as request and application forms, certificates of inheritance and in some cases an inventory list. Stichting Jokos was a collaboration of a number of Jewish organizations: Stichting Joods Maatschappelijk Werk (Jewish Social Work Foundation), Nederlands-Israëlitisch Kerkgenootschap (Dutch-Israeli Church Organization), Portugees-Israëlitische Gemeente (Portugese-Israeli Congregation), Liberaal Joodse Gemeente (Liberal Jewish Congregation), Stichting

Schadeloosstelling Joodse Oorlogsslachtoffers in Nederland (Foundation for Compensation of Jewish War Victims in the Netherlands). The Jokos archives are held by the Amsterdam Municipal Library and are the property of the Jewish Social Work Foundation (JMW).

Jewish children
An estimated six million Jews were murdered in an astonishingly horrific genocide during the Second World War. Among them were about one and a half million children. Children that otherwise would grow up to become the next generation of Jewish parents.

Jewish Council
During World War II, the Germans established Jewish councils, usually called Judenraete. These Jewish municipal administrations were required to ensure that Nazi orders and regulations were implemented. Jewish council members also sought to provide basic community services for ghettoized Jewish populations. Forced to implement Nazi policy, the Jewish councils remain a controversial and delicate subject. Jewish council chairmen had to decide whether to comply or refuse to comply with German demands to, for example, list names of Jews for deportation. In The Netherlands the Jewish council set up in February 1941 which had to govern the Jewish community in the Netherlands. The Nazi occupiers on February 12, 1941, ordered Asscher and Cohen to head up a new Jewish Counsel voor Amsterdam. This council was quickly granted authority over the entire Jewish community in the Netherlands. The occupier used to relay orders to the Jewish community and its leaders through the Jewish Council, which made the organization into a relay for anti-Jewish measures. The leaders of the Jewish Council were also deported to transit camp Westerbork in September 1943, which meant the de facto end of the council. Asscher survived his imprisonment at Bergen-Belsen and returned to Amsterdam after the conclusion of the war. Aside from historian David Cohen who also survived Theresienstadt concentration camp, all other members of the Jewish Council perished, including the Chief Rabbi of Amsterdam Lodewijk Sarlouis.

Kashrut
Is a set of Jewish religious dietary laws. Food that may be consumed according to *halakha* (Jewish law) is termed kosher (English, meaning 'fit'). Among the numerous laws that form part of *kashrut* are the prohibitions on the consumption of certain animals (such as pork, shellfish [both Mollusca and Crustacea], and most insects, with the exception of certain species of kosher locusts), mixtures of meat and milk, and the commandment to slaughter mammals and birds according to a process known as *shechita*. There are also laws regarding agricultural produce that might impact the suitability of food for consumption. Most of the basic laws of *kashrut* are derived from the Torah's Books of Leviticus and Deuteronomy. Their details and practical application, however, are set down in the oral law (eventually codified in the Mishnah and Talmud) and elaborated on in the later rabbinical literature.

Ketubah
This is a marriage certificate drawn up in Aramaic which in accordance to Jewish law must be signed by two witnesses and often also by the chatan (groom) and sets out the obligations of the groom towards the bride. At a Jewish wedding, the deed is often signed prior to the ceremony underneath the chuppah (Jewish marriage ceremony) and read out later during the ceremony. The Ketubah contains one of the oldest existing forms of alimony. By signing the deed, the man commits himself to provide for the upkeep of the wife by paying her a sum of money in case of a divorce. The text is more or less fixed and only the names of the couple, the date on which the deed is signed, and the special prenuptial agreements are added.

Kibbutz
A collective agricultural settlement in Israel. The first kibbutz, Degania Alef, was founded in 1910 by Jewish Palestinians, ten years before the start of the start of the British mandate over Palestine. The kibbutz was the pride of the socialist Jewish administration thanks to the far-reaching application of socialist principles, but also in comparison with the cooperative moshav. The ideological basis for the kibbutz model is a

concept of the 'industrial village', a small community in which industry and agriculture meet. Women were also used for heavy physical labor. From cloakrooms (in extreme cases) to the houses where people lived, almost everything was common property. Children had to sleep in children's homes from an early age. All meals were eaten together. Today, the level of collectivism in the kibbutz is drastically lower. Some kibbutz has completely eliminated the communal dining room. The cooperative company has been dissolved in a few kibbutzim, often due to debts. These kibbutzim have now often become 'ordinary' villages.

Kooi
The Kooi's were friends of my foster parents. They were one generation above us. Jan Dirk Kooi (1922-1991) and Jo (Johanna 1919-2013). Mr. Jan Dirk Kooi was the secretary of the District Court Judge in Sneek, Jewish, fully assimilated and part of the small Remonstrant community in Leeuwarden. He went into hiding during the war. His wife Jo, not Jewish but with Jewish ancestors in her family tree as became clear later, also went into hiding because she was in the resistance and feared discovery. Like so many others, sometimes decades later, Jan Kooi went back to his roots and sought to join the Jewish Congregation. Jo was very motivated to follow her husband, just like Ivonne. It was not easy for them and it took them years of uninterrupted studying without ever losing their intense interest in Judaism, Israel, its people, history and culture. The finally became members of a Liberal Jewish congregation.

Kosher
This concerns food. If food is kosher, it can be eaten by Jews. When is food kosher? There are three main rules. A dish or meal may not contain a combination of meat and milk or a derivative thereof (no sandwich with meat products and butter, or steak with a glass of milk). Another rule is that meat may come only from certain species (split-hoof ruminants such as beef, sheep and goats). Only certain fish species (with visible scales and fins) and certain bird species (such as chicken, turkey and goose) may be eaten. The third rules is that species that may be eaten, with the exception of fish species, must be butchered

in a certain way. Kosher, ritually approved, prepared according to Jewish food laws. Jewish law contains many regulations regarding the preparation and eating of food. They come from the Torah. The best-known rules are the ban on eating pork, eel and shellfish and the ban on eating milk and meat products at the same time. All these rules are taken into account in a kosher kitchen.

Landwacht
(National Watch Organization in the Nederland,) a paramilitary organization founded by the German occupying forces in 1943. They were mostly Dutch NSB* party members with a hunting rifle. They called them 'Jan Hagel'. Jan Hagel is a synonym for scum!

Le Dor Va Dor
'From generation to generation.' Judaism is a family connection, in the continuity from generation to generation. When we begin the Amidah, the main prayer of every service, we call God, 'our God and the God of our fathers and mothers.' We begin by reminding ourselves of our connection to all the generations who came before us and kept Judaism alive, who forged links in the chain of tradition and heritage. In that same prayer we also sing, *'Le-dor va-dor,'* meaning 'from generation to generation.' Judaism is much more than a religion in the sense of dogma and belief. It is a diverse religious civilization that offers us nearly forty centuries worth of deep wisdom, mind-expanding learning and meaning-making. Judaism is a heritage of deep spirituality, lively culture, social consciousness and a passion for justice. This family heritage belongs to us because our ancestors kept it alive against the odds, and yes, because they made their children do it, and thank G-d for that.

Leffring, Jetty
Her maiden name was Jetty Wiersma. Her Jewish name is Henriëtte Marianna Stouwer, born on 14 November 1942 in Amsterdam. She went into hiding as a baby at Mrs. And Mr. Trijntje and Sjoerd Wiersma in Joure. Friesland. After the war, Jetty visited her uncle and aunt Wiersma in Scharnegoutum, our neighbors. We were four

years old when we met for the first time. Jetty also had no idea she was Jewish. Her immediate family was murdered. Shortly before Jetty leaves primary school, she learns that she is Jewish. She becomes a member of the Reformed Church when she is eighteen. When Jetty marries Jille Leffring, she receives all existing information about her family from her foster parents. She is baptized together with her husband Jille in 1989.

Lennep
Hester Juliana Octavia van Lennep was the eighth child of an old aristocratic Amsterdam family of Reformed Christians, with seven much older siblings. During a vacation in Germany in the 1930s, she and her mother came face to face with Nazi propaganda. Hester's sister and her two grown-up sons were the key figures in the CS-6 Resistance group, named for their home address, Corellistraat 6. It was through them that around Christmas 1942 Hester met 42-year-old Sándor Baracs, a Hungarian Jew and one of the first Resistance workers. Before they met, Hester had helped a Jewish boy named Peter Frank find a place to hide. Hester and Sándor fell in love and decided to devote themselves to hiding Jewish children. Hester ran a skin care institute in Amsterdam, and the building became a place of transit for dozens of Jewish children who were then taken to hiding places by Hester or one of her associates. In early 1943 Hester and Sándor were approached by many desperate parents asking them to save their children. In May 1943 Hester and Sándor contacted Dr. Gesina van der Molen*, a member of the editorial staff of the illegal newspaper Trouw. Gesina knew many safe places where children could be hidden. Hester and Sándor joined the Trouw-group. Together with Gesina and other people, including Mien Bouwman, who accompanied many children to their hiding places, they arranged safe houses for between 80 and 100 children. Hester and Sándor were married in 1944 in the Tienhoven Town Hall in Utrecht, whose incumbent mayor had been appointed by Queen Wilhelmina. After the war many of the children they had saved came back to visit the Baracs family. On February 22,1981, Yad Vashem recognized Hester Juliana Octavia Baracs-van Lennep as Righteous Among the Nations.

Leopold, Ronald
He was the general secretary/director of the PUR until December 31, 2010. The Dutch Social Insurance Bank took over the implementation of the acts on January 1, 2011. The number of 'customers' of the PUR became too small. After having working for the PUR for twenty years, Mr. Leopold joined the Anne Frank Foundation as executive director on January 1, 2011.

Le-Ezrath Ha-Jeled
The 'Le-Ezrath Ha-Jeled' (Help the Child) foundation, a Jewish foundation, was concerned with the care of Jewish war foster children. As documents show, the foundation was primarily concerned with restoring the specifically Jewish character of the upbringing of these Jewish children who had often been exclusively in non-Jewish environments during the years of occupation. To this end, efforts were made to ensure that after the liberation the children would preferably be assigned to Jewish foster parents or homes. On more than one occasion, these efforts clashed with the government-established Commission for War Foster Children. In the course of 1950, 'Le-Ezrath Ha-Jeled' merged with three other Jewish institutions concerned with child care: the Bergstichting, (The Jewish boy house) and the S.A. Rudelsheimstichting. The foundation has been called 'Gefusioneerde Instellingen', (Fusionized Institutions) since then.
From: https://www.archieven.nl/nl/

Levite
A Levite assists an Aaronic priest with the slaughter of a Passover lamb (2 Chron. 30:16-17). A Levite (from Levi, 'attached') is a member of the Hebrew tribe of Levi in the Jewish tradition. The Levites served as assistants to the sons and descendants of the first chief priest, Aaron, at the Tabernacle in the wilderness and later at the Temple of Jerusalem. When the Israelites entered the land of Canaan, the Levites received no tribal land. Instead, they attended local altars, supervised cities of refuge, and served as judges and educators. In return, the members of the tribes with lands were expected to give tithes to the Levites and to provide them with local pastures on which to graze their own cattle.

LO
The Landelijke Organisatie voor Hulp aan Onderduikers (National Organization for Assistance to People in Hiding) was a Dutch resistance movement during the Second World War between mid-1942 and May 1945.

Mezuzah
A parchment scroll is rolled up, enclosed in a case of wood, metal or plastic material and attached to the doorpost. On the parchment are several passages from the Torah with the text of an important prayers. You can find a mezuzah at every right side of the doorpost in a Jewish house, except on rooms as toilets and bathrooms. Jews touch the mezuzah when entering a room and bring their fingers to their lips.

NSB
The Dutch Socialist Movement in the Netherlands (Dutch: *Nationaal-Socialistische Beweging in Nederland*, NSB) was a Dutch fascist and later national socialist political party. As a parliamentary party participating in legislative elections, the NSB had some success during the 1930s. It remained the only legal party in the Netherlands during most of the Second World War. In 1940 the German occupation government had outlawed all socialist and communist parties; in 1941 it forbade all parties, except for the NSB. The NSB openly collaborated with the occupation forces. Its membership grew to about 100,000. The NSB played an important role in lower government and civil service; every new mayor appointed by the German occupation government was a member of the NSB. Dutch Historians Lou de Jong and A.A. de Jonge have characterized NSB members as socially isolated opportunists who were motivated to join the NSB through a mix of opportunism, idealism and social connections. The term 'NSB'er' has become synonymous with traitor in the Netherlands, and is used as an insult, especially in the context of ratting somebody out to authorities. A grim joke after World War II, made by Dutch Resistance fighters, is that former NSB members insisted that their acronym actually stood for 'Niet So [zo] Bedoeld' or 'We didn't mean it' as they attempted to downplay their treachery.

NSDAP
The National Socialist German Workers' Party, generally known as the Nazi Party, was a very right-wing political party in Germany active between 1920 and 1945 which practiced the ideology of Nazism. (Source: Wikipedia)

Nursery
The nursery was located at Plantage Middenlaan 31, directly opposite the Hollandsche Schouwburg. This nursery, officially called 'Vereeniging Zuigelingen-Inrichting en Kinderhuis', (Society for Infants and Children's Home), was managed by Henriëtte Henriquez Pimentel (1876-1943) as of 1926. Both Jewish and non-Jewish children were placed and cared for at the nursery. The staff was also mixed. Young women could follow an internal training program to become a child nurse. During the war, in 1941, the non-Jewish personnel were dismissed after a German decree. In October 1942, the building was requisitioned as an annex to the Hollandsche Schouwburg and the function of the nursery changed. Jewish children up to thirteen years of age were separated from their parents in the Hollandsche Schouwburg. These children had to wait for deportation at the nursery. It was like a children's prison during that time. Due to the limited space in the Hollandsche Schouwburg, the German occupiers did not consider the building suitable to house children. They also thought that children would cause unrest. The Jewish staff in the nursery consisted of women aged about seventeen to twenty. It was hard for parents to be separated from their children, it was a relief that their children stayed in a somewhat child-friendly environment in the nursery and could play there. Parents and children were reunited again during the transports from the Hollandsche Schouwburg to the Central Station in Amsterdam, being transported to the transit camp Westerbork. From there they were waiting for the freight trains for deportation to the east.

On December 10, 1982, a bronze plaque was revealed in the wall of Plantage Middenlaan 27, formerly the Hervormde Kweekschool (The Protestant Teacher Collage). It contains the following text:

'To all who helped save Jewish children from deportation during the German occupation, 1940-1945'.
- the Jewish resistance in the Hollandsche Schouwburg;
- the Jewish staff of the nursery;
- the Kweekschool; (the Protestant Teacher Collage);
- the child rescuers;
- the thousands of people throughout the country who were involved in rescuing Jewish children;
- the foster families;
- people who arranged money and vouchers.

Oosterkamp, Hendrika (Hennie)
Opened the front door for an unknown Jewish baby. The future of the world depends on decisions that are taken in a second and my future depended on that one second when Hennie held the door open for me.

Orthodox
The term 'Orthodox' is not really correct because it gives the impression that there is a certain rigidity. However, there are developments that are based on following a certain tradition. The term traditional Judaism is better. Traditional Judaism cherishes and adheres to the letter of the Torah text and the increasingly developed and refined doctrine which is still based on the opinions formed in previous generations.

Polak, Bea and Wim
Bea Biet and Wim Polak married during the Second World War. They married under false names and received a false marriage permit. Their Jewish papers and those of many others were burned by the Dutch resistance during the war. They had great difficulties remarrying under their own names after the war. Their children are Simone (1946) and Inez (1949). Bea was the owner of the Jewish Bookstore Joachimstal from 1949 - 1969. *Bea Polak told me in the sixties that the Cosman's had agreed with the Rienstra's not to introduce me to my Jewish relatives who were still alive.* The Cosman's invited these family members and acquaintances of the Zwaaf-Godschalk family to come by in the

evening but I did not understand who these visitors were. I remember that these 'visits' were emotional and that the visitors would stare at me.

Rabbi
Trough his rigorous training he becomes an expert knowledge of the Torah, the Talmud, and the codes of Jewish Law. A rabbi is a Jewish scholar who is an expert in the field of halacha, the Jewish law. Literally, rabbi means teacher. The term rabbi is commonly used today to indicate the spiritual leader of a synagogue. The title of rabbi nowadays means 'Teacher in Talmudic Judaism'. Literature shows that the title was already in use during the 2nd Temple Period. The title of Rabbi is derived from the noun 'Rav' which means 'great' in Hebrew. This term does not appear as such in the Torah. The title only became common for Wise Men and Scholars around the beginning of the civil calendar.

Resistance
According to L. de Jong, approximately 25,000 illegal resistance fighters acted in a permanent organizational partnership until September 1944. This figure does not include individually operating resistance fighters, people in hiding, people who accepted people in hiding, and other helpers of the resistance who were not affiliated with an organization. The number of resistance fighters increased considerably as of September 1944. At the time of the liberation, approximately 60,000 people north of the rivers were part of the Internal Armed Forces (Dutch: Binnenlandse Strijdkrachten or BS). Not all of these 60,000 members had actually carried out illegal work in a narrower sense before the liberation. De Jong estimates that the total number of resistance fighters, or illegal workers as he defines them, was approximately 45,000 throughout the entire occupation period.

(L. de Jong, Het Koninkrijk der Nederlanden in de Tweede Wereldoorlog, section 10b (The Hague 1981) page 744-746).

Rienstra, Feike
My foster father as of November 8, 1945. A man with good intentions but with a problematic character. He had difficulty accepting my presence. This must have caused major problems in his marriage and indirectly also for me.

Sabbath
Sabbath, Hebrew Shabbat, (from *shavat*, 'cease,' or 'desist'). The time division follows the biblical story of creation: 'And there was evening and there was morning, one day' (Genesis 1:5). The Torah begins with a description of the creation. It states that G'd, after creating men on the sixth day, rested on the seventh day. In memory of this, the seventh day of the week, the Saturday, is a rest day called the Sabbath. Jews do not work or go to school. Nor do Jews create anything on this day, just like G'd. This 'not creating anything' has far-reaching consequences due to which Jews are unable to many things you may initially expect they still could do. In essence, the Sabbath day is a withdrawal from your daily life to instead focus fully on the special, the sublime, the uncommon. This mental release is compared to the liberation of the Jews from Egyptian slavery. Not only a physical liberation but also a liberation from Egyptian thinking. The Sabbath begins at dusk on Friday and ends twenty-five hours later on Saturday evening. At home, two candles are lit, and the day is consecrated by saying a prayer and drinking a cup of wine. This is followed by the meal which begins with cutting one of the two prepared braided breads. This bread is called challah. The next day, two meals with bread are eaten again on the next day. Sabbath is a day of rest in memory of the seventh day of creation when G'd rested. There is a general abstention from work, which implies a ban on making fire, cooking, carrying things, trading, and spending or receiving money. The food, which is prepared in advance, is kept warm in a so-called Sabbath oven.

Second World War
The most serious form of anti-Semitism occurred at the time of the regime of the German National Socialists led by Hitler. First in Germany, from 1938 in Austria, later in Poland and all countries

conquered by Hitler-Germany during the Second World War, including The Netherlands. The German State attacked other states aimed to exterminate a number of population groups in its own country and in the occupied states, particularly the Jewish population. A total of approximately six million Jews were systematically separated from their non-Jewish peers, gathered and transported to concentration and extermination camps where they were murdered in the most efficient manner. The Germans received help from the local population of the countries they had conquered.

Shiva
Means: 'sitting' during the week of mourning. The week of mourning begins after the funeral, which is the most intensive period of mourning called Shiva (which means seven). This is why this week is called 'sitting shiva'. People go to the house of mourning after the funeral. The mirrors are covered here, which is a tradition of unknown origin. When the mourners arrives home, they light a candle or special lamp, called ner neshama. 'Light of the soul' which will stay on all week. A simple meal is eaten, often bread and egg. The mourners sit on low chairs. The mourners always wear the same clothes with a ritual tear. Men do not shave, and women do not wear make-up. People often do not wear any shoes or leather shoes. They do not work during the week of mourning. No music is played. The mourners do not have to be polite or hospitable. The visitors take care of the food.

Shoah
The Holocaust, also referred to as the Shoah, was a genocide during World War II in which Nazi Germany, aided by its collaborators, systematically murdered some six million European Jews, around two-thirds of the Jewish population of Europe, between 1941 and 1945. Jews were targeted for extermination as part of a larger event involving the persecution and murder of other groups, including in particular the Roma and sick', as well as ethnic Poles and other Slavs, Soviet citizens, Soviet prisoners of war, political opponents, gay men and Jehovah's Witnesses, resulting in up to 17 million murders overall. The persecution and murder of Jews during the Second World

War. The Hebrew word Shoah literally means: 'catastrophe', disaster and 'destruction'. The systematic persecution of the Jews and their destruction by the Nazis is also called the Holocaust. This is factually incorrect because the word Holocaust has a different meaning. The actual persecution and destruction of Jews would more accurately be referred to as Shoah. The Jews use the term Shoah, which is Hebrew for 'destruction' or 'disaster'. A disaster is something that happens to you. 'Holocaust', on the other hand, comes from Greek and means 'sacrifice', which is something that can be demanded from or imposed on you. A sacrifice can also be made voluntarily. Because of this last meaning, Jews prefer to speak of the Shoah.

Sobibor
This destruction camp is known for the uprising that took place among the prisoners, an unparalleled phenomenon in the history of the Nazi concentration and extermination camps. A resistance group was formed under the leadership of Leon Feldhendler and Aleksandr Petjerski in the summer of 1943. This group organized an uprising on 14 October of that year, killing ten Germans, two Volksdeutsche and eight trawnikis. 365 prisoners managed to flee the camp and most of them were murdered during the manhunt that followed. Most Jews who had stayed behind in the camp were shot. The order came to shoot the remaining Jews in November. The Polish people who lived near the camp dug up the entire camp after the war looking for valuables buried by the prisoners. They found a lot of wedding rings and other jewelry. The platform, the Chelm-Wlodawa railway line and the home of the camp commander remained of camp Sobibor. No barracks, no gas chamber or barbed wire. We walked to a place with an artificial hill. People had created a hill made of holy ashes of those who were murdered in the gas chamber and then burned. Cremation is not common in the Jewish tradition. Jewish graves may not be cleared, and Jewish cemeteries must remain intact forever.

The Sobibor Foundation in The Netherlands was founded in 1999 by Jules Schelvis, the only Dutch survivor of the 14th transport to the extermination camp Sobibor. Jules Schelvis (7 January 1921-3 April

2016) was a Dutch historian, writer, Sobibor Holocaust survivor, and Nazi hunter. He lost his wife and most of his family during The Holocaust. Schelvis was a plaintiff and expert witness during the trial of John Demjanjuk.

Süskind
Walter Süskind (born in Germany in 1906 – murdered in Polen in 1945) was a Jewish German of partly Dutch origin. He was a member of the Dutch Jewish council (Dutch: *Joodsche Raad*) during the Second World War. Walter Süskind was the director of the Hollandsche Schouwburg, had helped about 600 Jewish children to escape the persecution of the Jews.

In 1944, Süskind, his wife and his daughter were sent to the transit camp Westerbork. Due to his good relations with the SS leadership of the Hollandsche Schouwburg, he could return to Amsterdam, but he eventually went back to his family in Westerbork. He also wanted to let people escape from this transit camp. His wife and daughter were murdered in an extermination camp, they were sent to. Walter Süskind was murdered on 28 February 1945 at an unknown location in central Europe during the death marches. On 19 January 2012, the Dutch movie *Süskind* was released. This movie is based on the life of Walter Süskind A book titled 'Süskind' written by Dutch author Alex van Galen (in Dutch) described Walter Süskinds life. If my absence had been discovered, my parents might have been shot on the spot. At the very last moment, shortly before their deportation to transit camp Westerbork, they committed an act of heroic assistance by letting me go into hiding by accepting the proposal of Walter Süskind, the director of the Hollandsche Schouwburg. This must have been an intensely sad decision with a grief that cannot be expressed in words. After first having had to bury their daughter, they now had to give away their son. My parents gave me a chance to survive and live for a second time.

Synagogue
'Assembly', Hebrew: *bet kenesset*, 'house of assembly' or *bet tefila*, 'house of prayer', Yiddish: *shul*, Ladino: *esnoga* or *kahal*), is a Jewish house of

worship. Synagogues have a large place for prayer (the main sanctuary) and may also have smaller rooms for study and sometimes a social hall and offices. Some have a separate room for Torah study, called the *beth midrash* 'house of study'. Synagogues are consecrated spaces used for the purpose of prayer, Tanakh* (the entire Hebrew Bible, including the Torah) reading, study and assembly; however, a synagogue is not necessary for worship. Halakha holds that communal Jewish worship can be carried out wherever ten Jews (a minyan) assemble. Worship can also be carried out alone or with fewer than ten people assembled together. However, halakha considers certain prayers as communal prayers and therefore they may be recited only by a minyan. In terms of its specific ritual and liturgical functions, the synagogue does not replace the long-since destroyed Temple in Jerusalem.

Szenes

Channa (1921-1944) was a poet and Special Operations Executive (SOE) paratrooper. She was one of 37 Jewish parachutists of Mandate Palestine parachuted by the British Army into Yugoslavia during the Second World War to assist in the rescue of Hungarian Jews about to be deported to the German death camp at Auschwitz. Szenes was arrested at the Hungarian border, then imprisoned and tortured, but refused to reveal details of her mission. Channa was executed by a German firing squad on November 7, 1944. She is regarded as a national heroine in Israel, where her poetry is widely known and the headquarters of the Zionist youth movements *Israel Hatzeira*, a kibbutz and several streets are named after her.

Talmud

The Talmud (written teachings) follows the pattern of Mishna (oral teaching). Each paragraph in the Mishna is discussed by scholars in the Talmud. The Talmud resembles the minutes of a discussion in this sense. The discussion is sometimes very broad, and a number of cases may be involved that at first sight have nothing to do with it, but which do belong to the topics to be discussed as a form of associative thinking.

Tanakh

Is an acronym of the first Hebrew letter of each of the Masoretic Text's three traditional subdivisions: Torah ('Teaching', also known as the Five Books of Moses), Nevi'im ('Prophets') and Ketuvim ('Writings') hence TaNaKh. The books of the Tanakh were passed on by each generation and, according to rabbinic tradition, were accompanied by an oral tradition, called the Oral Torah. The three-part division reflected in the acronym 'Tanakh' is well attested in the literature of the Rabbinic period. During that period, however, 'Tanakh' was not used. Instead, the proper title was Mikra meaning is 'reading' or 'that which is read', because the biblical texts were read publicly. Mikra continues to be used in Hebrew to this day, alongside Tanakh, to refer to the Hebrew scriptures. In modern spoken Hebrew, they are interchangeable.

Torah

The Torah is a five-part book that has two elements: a history starting at the creation of heaven and earth until the death of Moshe just before the Jewish people enter the land of Canaan after being rescued from Egypt and making a forty-year journey through the desert. In addition to this 'storyline', the books also contain obligations. The Torah is also called the Teachings or the Law because of this. Thora is a Hebrew word that means 'education'. Often it is translated with 'law', but that translation is limited. The Torah is much more for the Jewish people than a collection of rules. The Torah is formed by the first five books of the Bible: (the italic words are the original Hebrew names) Genesis – Bresjiet, Exodus – Sjemot, Leviticus – Wajikra, Numeri – Bemidbar Deuteronomy – Dewariem, in addition to the many prescriptions, the Torah also includes the creation story (Genesis) and the exodus of the Israelites from Egypt (Exodus). After the Hebrew people had come out of Egypt and were on their way to the Promised Land, they received from God at Mount Sinai the Torah. How many commandments are there in the Torah? In total there are 613 injunctions and prohibitions in the Torah. In Judaism these are called mitzvot. It concerns 248 commandments and 365 prohibitions. A command is something you have to do, while a prohibition is something that you should not do.

Because the word Torah is often translated 'law,' it has been given a negative meaning for non-Jews. That while Jews themselves regard the Torah as a gift from God. In Judaism there is even a special feast to celebrate that God has given the Torah: Simchat Torah (in Dutch: Joy of Law). This festival celebrates Jews every year. The Torah books I use has been translated into Dutch by Jitschak Dasberg.

Ulpan
An institute for the intensive study of Hebrew. It is the Hebrew word for 'studio', 'training' or 'instruction'. The ulpan is designed to teach adults in Israel the basic skills of speaking and writing the language. Most ulpanim also give instructions in the foundations of Israeli culture, history and geography. The main goal of the ulpan is to help new citizens integrate into the social, cultural and economic life of their new country as well and as quickly as possible.

Z"L"
Blessed Memory

Zwaaf, Barend
After my meeting with Mr. Barend Zwaaf, during the life broadcast on TV in 1994, he took me to the places in Amsterdam where my family members had lived before, they were arrested and deported. I walked where the footsteps of my relatives. It was an emotional experience. Barend Zwaaf also had his own footsteps in Amsterdam. He was born there on December 25, 1921 and died in Amsterdam on July 9, 2016. His family had a store in sour food products. They would originally sell these on the street and would later also pickle food themselves and deliver these to other stores and sandwich and meat shops. They were successful, had their own business premises and finally exported to Belgium, Sweden and England. The crisis of the 1930s hit the trade and the war and occupation dealt the Jewish company the final blow. However, they could still sell things on the street like they used to. But the streets were not safe. It only took something to happen, like a riot or a fight, and the Germans intervened. The Grüne Polizei haphazardly collected identity documents that had to be collected

from the offices of the Ortskommandant (District Commander) from 20.00 o'clock in the evening. Street sellers, on the move, were always targeted. Barend was one of the Jews who would regularly be beaten up. When he reported for the first time, he was immediately hit on the nose with brass knuckles and started to bleed. He was locked up in a cellar for a few days and abused. Barend Zwaaf married Sonja van Cleef in 1942. The bride and groom with bridal bouquet, floral corsage and a Jewish badge. More and more people in their vicinity were getting arrested and would disappear, including family members: Sonja her parents and both brothers, Barend his father and mother. Barend received a 'Sper' because he would can vegetables that were sent to the Westerbork and Vught camps. But this was only temporary; he was arrested in his wedding year and deported together with Sonja to Auschwitz. His young wife was murdered there in 1945. Barend survived seventeen concentration camps.

Index of names

Aagje (Abma) 166
Aagje (Rienstra 'aunt') 40
Abma 42, 135, 166, 167
Abram Abram 166
Abram Ans 166
Abram H. 166
Abram L.H. 167
Abram Max 6, 42, 63, 64, 69, 70, 133, 135, 166, 167
Abram R.M. 167
Ady (Godschalk) 77, 133, 135
Agsteribbe-Zwaaf M. 68
Aliyah 9, 62, 81, 112, XXX, 130, 131, 133, 138, 178
Amen 105, 146, 147, 149, 178
Amram (Levite) 144
Anna (Godschalk-Zwaaf, mother) 16, 28, 95-98, 103, 107, 128, 163, 173, 184, 185
Anna (sister of grandmother) 128
Anna Vanessa 9, 71, 72, 75-79, 82, 83, 84, 86, 131, 132, 133, 135, 144, 146, 182
Anti-Semitism 130, 151, 153, 154, 158, 179, 185, 199
Apeldoorn 57
Arjeh (Lion Patrick) 182
Arnhem 53
Artis (Zoo) 17
Asscher A. 198

Atema 43-45
Auschwitz 5, 90, 96, 100-102, 104, 106-108, 125, 130, 164, 165, 169, 170, 179, 180, 203, 206, 209
Aviva (Godschalk) 82

B"H 7, 182
Baarda, (book shop) 40, 49
Baarsma L. 50
Babylonian Talmud 132
Bajema H. 42
Baracs S. 18, 19, 24-26, 32, 33, 67, 160, 161, 180, 181, 193
Beekhuis mr. 50, 60
Beem D. van 164
Beem Ester-Zwaaf van 165
Beem J. van 165
Ben Gurion D. 77
Ben Zion Ben Arjeh 84, 182
Berg J. van der 48
Beth Din 84, 181, 182, 186
Bierenbroodspot A. 114
Biet B. 197
Blok-Blitz 6, 23, 26-31, 84, 171, 175
Blom H. 100
Boas A. 64, 67
Boas D. 64, 67
Boas H. 99
Boaz 81

Boeken-Velleman L. 100, 101
Boer de K. de 70
Boersma Eelke 143
Boersma Eelkje 13, 14, 38
Boersma R. (Oosterkamp) 13, 143, 151
Boersma Th. 14
Boetje H. 50
Boissevain 180
Bolt D. 93
Boorsma E. 143
Boorsma Koos 81, 94, 117, 120, 122, 123, 133-135, 143
Boorsma Sj. 94, 143
Boot Ids 90, 183
Boot J. 183
Bootsma Ger 143
Bootsma Gosse 143
Bosecker K. 51, 184
Bouman M. 20, 23
Bounty hunters (kopgeld) 17, 183
Brandon J. 165
Bratzlav N. van 63
Brozin 86
Brucht (Rienstra) 40
Burg A. 131
Busschbach T. 57
BVL 14

C&A 50, 70, 176, 184
CADSU 48, 186
Cahan J. 106
Cate L. ten 100
Chaim (Eduth) 82
Channa (Anna Vanessa) 182
Channa (Wetberg) 47
Chasing trails 5, 92

Child Protection Board in Amsterdam 163
Child rescuers 18, 183, 197
Chuppah 16, 26, 29, 84, 132, 182, 184, 185, 190
Citroen M. 163, 209
Civitavecchia 61
Clothing Company Max Abram 63, 64, 70, 134, 166, 167
Cohen D. 198
Cohen E. 76, 182
Cohen E. van der Spiegel 108, 110
Cohen J. 107
Cohen L. 80
Cohen R. 113, 114
Cohen S. 109
Cornelia (Graeve de) 134
Cornelia (sister) 16, 18, 128, 164
Cornelis Tr. 92
Cosman Bettie 17, 34, 49, 54, 64, 66, 97, 98, 184, 185
Cosman Betty 167, 168
Cosman S. 17, 34, 50, 53, 60, 63, 93, 167, 184, 197, 198
Cunaeus P. 94

Damsma 38
Dasberg Ch. 112, 113
Dasberg J. 205
Dasberg N. 82, 112, 113, 182
Daum A. 131
De Wittenberg 55, 56
Dekker J. 42, 166
Demjanuk J. 202
Demnig G. 125-127
Dijkstra G & G. 122, 143

Dijkstra K. 20, 151
Donin H.H. 210
Donner J. 160
Drachten 77
Drenkelford H. 168
Dresden S. 167
Dutch Auschwitz Committee/
 Netherlands Auschwitz Comite
 (NAC) 90, 100, 106, 169, 179, 209
Dutch Orthodox Calvinistic Church 47,
 63
Duveen-Frank J. 23, 68

Eddy (Boorsma) 143
Eelke (Boorsma) 143
Eelkje (Boorsma) 13, 14, 38
El Male Rachamiem 103, 185
Ephraim 139, 140
Eric (Boorsma) 143
Euphonia 47
Evers-Emden B. 91, 163, 208
Excelsior 41

Flim B.J. 163, 208
France Louise-Maria de 91
Frank A. 101, 194, 210
Frank E. 101
Frank M. 101
Frank P. 193
Fred (Graeve de) 58
Friedman-van der Heide R. 32

Geens J. van 100
Gelderman H. 55
Gerrie 21
Gerrit 13, 20-24, 26, 27, 34, 124, 151

Gerritse-Aldewereld J. 68
Giyur 185
Glasius L. 100
Godschalk B.V. (LTD) 77, 80
Godschalk A. (my mother) 28, 98, 103,
 107
Godschalk C. (my sister) 16, 18, 128, 164
Godschalk H (my aunt) 103, 163
Godschalk J. 68
Godschalk L. (my grandfather) 7, 15, 17,
 19, 20, 22, 23, 28, 94, 95, 103, 108,
 128, 163, 171, 185, 186, 197
Godschalk L. (my father) 12, 16, 20, 22,
 23, 28, 94, 96, 98, 103, 108, 128, 163,
 184-186, 197
Godschalk L. (my nephew), 103
Godschalk S. 82
Godschalk-Jacobs C. (my grandmother)
 7, 12, 16, 17, 19, 23, 95, 103, 108, 163
Goot A. van der 35
Goot G. van der 34
Goot L. van der 34, 35
Goot van der 20, 34, 151
Graatsma 22
Grishaver J. 6, 90, 100, 106, 169, 170
Grishaver L. 100, 169
Groen-Aldewereld 68
Groen-Aldewereld Sch. 68
Groeneveld E. Kuiper 123, 124, 142, 143
Groningen 49-52, 57, 70, 167, 172
Groot I. de 72

Haan F. 42, 143
Haan P. De 126
Harari 62
Hartmann H. jr. 68

Hartog B. 109
Heeg 34, 116-118, 141
Hema 51, 52, 63
Hendrika (Godschalk) 20, 103, 164
Hendriksen G. 50
Hendriksma D. 143
Herman S. 100, 102-104, 107
Herzliya 86, 87, 113
Hessel E. 143
Hiegentlich 63
Hilbrand (Abma) 166
Hitler A. 33, 154, 180, 199, 200, 204
Hofstra K. 15
Hogeweg 40
Hollandsche Schouwburg 12, 17-19, 68, 96, 107, 127, 150, 151, 183, 196, 197, 202
Hoop H. 19, 20, 164, 172
Hoop L. de (my nephew) 164
Houten B.W. van 160

Icodo 89, 210
Idor (Elazar) 77, 133, 135
Iron (Elazar) 77, 133, 135
Ivonne 9-11, 34, 57-59, 61, 63-67, 69-82, 84, 87, 93, 94, 100, 105, 111, 117, 120, 121, 123, 127, 131-135, 137, 140, 144, 145, 151, 171, 175, 177, 182, 191

Jacob (Graeve de) 58, 75, 134
Jacobs E. 68
JCC (Jewish Coordination Committee) 161
Jellema A. 42, 143
Jellema B. 41

Jellema K. 41, 42
Jew hunters 17, 183
Jewish Children 23, 32, 33, 90, 141, 145, 158-163, 181, 189, 193, 194, 196, 197, 202
Jewish Council 189
Jitschak (Godschalk) 82
JMW 89, 111, 114, 115, 187, 189
JNF 74, 75, 188
Joachimstal 54, 197
Joffer 65, 98
Jokos 50, 188, 189
Jong L. 195, 198
Jong S. de 166
Jonge A.A. 195
Joodsche Schouwburg 17
Joseph 139, 140, 152
Joseph Ch. 114
Jukema 14

Kaddish 16, 101, 105, 107, 109, 142, 146, 148, 149, 185
Kalma J.J. 162
Kattenburg S. 18
Kempe G. 157, 160
Ketubah 85, 190
Kfar Batja 82, 83
Kibbutz 61, 63, 82, 173, 190, 191, 203
King David 81, 140, 187
Kooi Jan en Jo 84, 191
Koopmans J. 42, 167
Krabbé J. 107
Kreisberg G. 111, 113, 114
Kreisberg P. 111
Kuiper-Groeneveld E. 123, 124, 142, 143

L.O./National Organization for Assistance to People in Hiding 13, 37, 195
Laan-Droogsma A. van der 143
Labour Council 37
Landwacht 192
Lange L. de 210
Le Dor Va Dor 73, 77, 139, 140, 192
Leeuwarden 13, 47, 46, 48, 50-53, 59, 63, 66, 70-72, 76, 81, 83, 118, 122, 182, 183, 191
Leeuwen H.G.A. van 20
Leeuwen H.L. van 20
Le-Ezrath Ha-Jeled 31, 32, 161, 194
Leffring Jetty 90, 192, 193
Leffring Jille 193
Lennep H.J.O. van 18, 67, 68, 151, 180, 193
Leopold R. 100, 194
Levite 144, 195
Libeskind D. 170
Light Air Target Artillery Division 55
LILOU 72
Lion (Godschalk, my father) 7, 16, 28, 72, 95, 96, 98, 103, 108, 164, 173, 174, 185
Lion Patrick 9, 71, 72, 78, 79, 82-85, 131-133, 135, 144, 146, 181, 182
Litsenburg-Jacobs W. van 23-25, 66, 68, 98
Little Jew 15, 39, 40
LO 13, 37, 195
Loekie 25-29, 32, 39, 41, 43-46
Loënga 36
Louis Godschalk & Zn. 95, 96

Majdanek 102, 104
Mama (my foster mother) 6, 13-15, 36, 37, 38, 40, 42, 44, 45, 59, 66, 70, 72, 75, 79, 84, 87, 116, 118, 120, 122-124, 133, 134, 143, 144, 146-148, 150-152, 156
Mantelhuis (Godschalk) 34, 69, 70, 72, 135, 167
Mantelhuis (Max Abram) 64, 167
Marjan 57
Mastenbroek 14
Mazirel L. 157, 160
Mediterranean Sea Towers 121, 136
Meerburg P. 157, 160
Meerschwam C. 177
Meerschwam J. 176,
Meerschwam S. 6, 72, 176, 177
Meijer G.M. 23, 24
Meinsma S. and P. 38
Memorial Avenue of Sobibor 105, 107, 108
Menasheh 139, 140
Mentz/Menat M. van 92, 94
Mezuzah 67, 195
Mikado's 47
Mishnah 190, 203
Molen G. van der 157, 160, 161, 193
Moses 94, 124, 130, 132, 144, 204
Moshav 62, 190
Moshe 28, 204
Mulder D. 106
Mulder S.I. 94
Mulder-Alderwereld H. 68
Mundstück J. 54, 56, 61, 62, 133, 151

Na'an 61
Nachum S. 63
Nadav M. and Z. 82
Naomi 80
Nes Ammim 62, 63,
Netanya 80
Neuteboom A. 100
Newman 210
NIW 98
Nordiya 121, 136
NSB 168, 192, 195
NSDAP 125, 196
Nursery 18-20, 68, 183, 196, 197

Oosterkamp (Hofstra) Klaske 15, 38
Oosterkamp Eke 13, 145
Oosterkamp fam. 13-15, 36-38, 124, 127, 135, 141, 144
Oosterkamp Hendrika (Hennie) (my mama) 6, 13, 20-23, 26, 78, 134, 143, 151, 166, 197
Oosterkamp K. 13-15, 78, 79, 143-145, 150, 151, 156
Oosterkamp M. 13, 145, 146
Oosterkamp N. 20
Oosterkamp R. 151
Oosterkamp S. 13, 145, 146
OPK (Oorlogs Pleeg Kinderen/ Commission for War Foster Children) 15, 19-24, 26-34, 68, 92, 97, 98, 128, 161-163, 180, 194
Orthodox 28, 31-33, 47, 53, 59, 62, 77, 131, 132, 163, 182, 186, 198, 197
Osnat 140
Osnat Bat Ya'cov (Ivonne) 84, 140, 182
Ossendrecht 52

Oswiecim 101, 180
Oudkerk B. 18

Palte H. 97, 98
Palte R. 98
Palte-Lazeron S. 94, 97
Pareira 158
Peters M. 107
Petter D. 94, 98
Philips F. 18
Pierik P. 134
Pierik W. Sr. 134
Pimentel H.H. 18, 196
Platein and the Ielanen 143
Polak B. 54, 134, 197
Polak F. 106
Polak G.I. 94
Polak W. 134, 197
Poland 100-102, 169, 170, 180, 199
Praag M. van 107
Professional School for the Retail 49, 52
Protestant Teacher Collage 18, 68, 122, 196, 197
Prummel 51
PUR 100-113, 114, 194

Queen 32, 170, 193

Ra'anana 82, 84, 86, 87, 181
Rabbi 198
Ramallah 85
Rasterhoff 70
Réaumurstraat 12, 65, 94-97, 127
Ree H. van 167
Regina (Eduth) 82
Rehoboth school 43

Resistance 198
Rienstra Baukje 143
Rienstra F. (foster father) 26-32, 34, 78, 118, 141, 144, 151, 199
Rienstra family 24, 26-35, 122, 124, 197
Rienstra Feike (cousin of my foster father) 40
Rienstra G. (son of Gerlof and Eke Rienstra) 122, 143
Rienstra Gerlof (husband of 'aunt' Eke Oosterkamp) 116
Rienstra K. 143
Rienstra L. 27, 32, 44, 46,
Rienstra Tj. 36
Rienstra-Bootsma Tr. 36, 38
Rienstra-Oosterkamp Eke 116, 117, 122, 143,145
Rienstra-Oosterkamp H. (foster mother) 6, 24, 27, 77-79, 132, 141, 142, 144, 150, 151
Rijkens 78
Rika (Godschalk) 171, 172
Rob (Graeve de) 58, 94
Ronn E. 153
Roos S. 210
Ross-Van Dorp C. 106
Rotary 86
Rozendaal D. 42
Rupp 59
Ruth 80

Sabbath 199
Sanders G.T.B. 210
Sarlou L. 189
Schaap J. 142

Scharnegoutum 5, 12-14, 20, 22, 23, 29, 36, 38, 39, 42, 47, 49, 63, 118, 123, 141, 143, 151, 166, 192
Schellings J.G. 95
Schelvis J. 100, 201, 202
Sealtiel S. 161
Seesing 72
Shazar Z. 131
Shelef N. 62
Shelef S. 59, 62
Shiraz (Godschalk) 77, 133, 135
Shiva 200
Shoah 8, 9, 82, 89, 99, 104, 130, 154, 169, 200, 201
Siegel Cohen van der E. 108, 110
Sivan G. 210
Slagter 53, 54, 56, 57, 133
Smit H. 134
Sneek 13, 20, 23, 34, 36, 40, 43, 60, 69-72, 75, 77, 81, 83, 90, 118, 122, 151, 166, 183, 191
Sobibor 19, 96, 100, 104, 105, 107-109, 146, 164, 165, 169, 201, 202
Sobibor Foundation 107, 201
Spier 98
Spoorloos (Chasing trails) 92, 93, 98, 99, 128
Stellingwerf-Elzinga 143
Stiens 72, 76, 111, 119, 122
Stolpersteine 5, 125, 126
Stouwer H.M. 192
Stroop 13, 20, 22
Süskind W. 18, 67, 68, 183, 202, 210
Synagogue 202
Szenes Channa 146, 203

Tal J. 160
Talma State 34, 116, 122, 123, 143
Talmud 149, 190, 198, 203
Talmud Thora School 54, 56, 62, 76, 151
Tanach 204
Tellegen 160
Tenkink J.C. 160
The Hidden Children Conference 89, 183
The Hidden Children Movement 89
Thijn E. van 89
Thomas (Boersma) 13, 14
Tiemersma L. 47
Tietjerk 71, 72
Tonny (Graeve de) 94
Torah 204
Trouw-verzetsgroep 18, 68, 160, 193

Ulpan 82, 205
Ulpan Akiva 80
Urim 82
Utrecht 52, 53, 55, 153, 160, 193, 209

Vandormaël H. van 134, 210
Velde-Rienstra M. van der 143
Velde S. van der 143
Verhey E. 210
Verkade 79
Vertegaal P.J. 92
Vischjager D.W. 183
Vlap-Botsma T. 143
Vlap A. 143
Vogel D. 84, 182
Vorst I. 210
Vos I. 102

Waard A. 157, 160
Wallenberg R. 87
Walzer 62
Wartman M. 92-94
Waterman J. 100
Waterman-Geens Judith 100, 105
Werkman W. 92
Werner Keller 153
Wertheim 100
Westerbork 12, 17, 19, 96, 97, 103, 106-109, 150, 169, 189, 196, 202, 206
Westerwereld-Aldewereld M. 68
Wetberg M. 46
Wetering N. van de 78, 84
Wiersma G.F. 14, 20, 24, 192
Wiersma J. 192
Wiersma P. 42
Wiersma Sj. 14, 90, 192
Wiersma Tr. 192
Wittenberg 55, 56
Wolf D.L. 210
WUV 111, 113, 114
Wytzes 39, 40

Ya'acov 139, 140
Yad Vashem 6, 74, 75, 77-79, 84, 87, 123, 141, 142, 144, 150, 152-156, 193
Yannay Y. 92-94

Z"L 205
Zijlstra A. 143
Zondervan-Rienstra J. 145
Zondervan Sj. 143
Zwaaf A. (sister of grandmother) 128
Zwaaf Anna (my mother) 16, 95, 103, 107, 128, 164, 184

Zwaaf B. 94, 205, 206
Zwaaf C. 68
Zwaaf C. (my niece) 103
Zwaaf family 6, 7, 23, 28, 30, 96, 108, 164, 184, 185, 197
Zwaaf H. (my grandfather) 7, 96, 102, 164
Zwaaf H. (my nephew) 102
Zwaaf H. (my uncle) 17
Zwaaf I. (administrator) 23, 30, 31, 68
Zwaaf I. (my nephew) 165
Zwaaf J. 68
Zwaaf L. (my aunt) 103, 128, 164
Zwaaf L. (my uncle) 102, 165
Zwaaf S. (my uncle) 103, 165
Zwaaf W. 68
Zwaaf-Aldewereld R. (Chelly) 68, 102, 164
Zwaaf-Stoete L. 68
Zwaaf-van Beem E. 103, 165
Zwaaf-van Cleef S. 206
Zwaaf-Zwaaf C (my grandmother) 7, 96, 102, 128, 164
Zwette (canal) 13, 14, 36, 38, 124, 166

Consulted sources

Auschwitz bulletin	Quarterly magazine of the Dutch Auschwitz Committee
Bert Jan Flim	Omdat hun hart sprak. Uitgeverij Kok Kampen Saving the children. CDL Press. Bethesda, Maryland Onder de klok. Georganiseerde hulp aan Joodse kinderen Gibbon Uitgeefagentschap
Bloeme Evers-Emden:	Onderduikouders en hun Joodse 'kinderen' over de onderduikperiode (1988) Geschonden bestaan: gesprekken met vervolgde Joden die hun kinderen moesten 'wegdoen' (1996) Als een pluisje in de wind (autobiografie, 2012) Ondergedoken geweest, een afgesloten verleden?: Joodse 'kinderen' over hun onderduik: vijftig jaar later Je ouders delen: een eerste onderzoek naar de gevoelens van eigen kinderen in pleeggezinnen in de oorlog en nu (1999)
Citroen Michal:	U wordt door niemand verwacht, Uitgeverij Het Spectrum. Utrecht See Gottschalk (must be Godschalk) pages 200, 201, 205, 210, 211, 212, 213, 215, 216, 217, 221, 222, 223, 224, and 225
Dahlby Frithiof:	Bijbels woordenboek 9de druk. Ten Have. Baarn

De crèche 1942-1943: Vrij Nederland januari 18, 1986

Diane L. Wolf:	Beyond Anne Frank. University of California Press. Berkeley. Los Angelos. Londen
Elma Verhey:	Kind van de rekening. Het Joods rechtsherstel van de Joodse oorlogswezen
Herman Vandormael:	Verborgen Oorlogsjaren Kinderen van Theresienstadt
Icodo	Geleende kinderen: ervaringen van onderduikouders en hun Joodse beschermelingen in de jaren 1942 tot 1945 (1994)
Rabbi Hayim Halevi Donin:	To be a Jew
Rabbijn ing. I. Vorst	Badèrech, op weg naar praktisch Joods leven
Dr. L. De Lange Dhr. S. Roos Dr. G.T.B. Sanders	Nederlands-Israëlisch Kerkgenootschap, Amsterdam
Walter Süskind Stichting Amsterdam:	De geschiedenis van de redding van Joodse kinderen 1942-1943
Wikipedia	
Yacov Newman, Judaism A-Z. Gavriel Sivan:	Lexicon of concepts & terms. Department for Torah Education and Culture in the Diaspora of the World Zionist Organization. Jerusalem